Tom - 9.7.99

If friends were flowers,
You'd be a rose!

Love "H"

The KALAHARI

SURVIVAL IN A THIRSTLAND WILDERNESS

DEDICATION

*Not only is the Kalahari Gemsbok National Park a very
special place, the people who work there are very special too.
I wish to dedicate this book to the staff of the Kalahari Gemsbok
National Park who, despite the considerable logistical difficulties
encountered in such a remote area, run this park
with such care and devotion.*

NIGEL DENNIS

The
KALAHARI

SURVIVAL IN A THIRSTLAND WILDERNESS

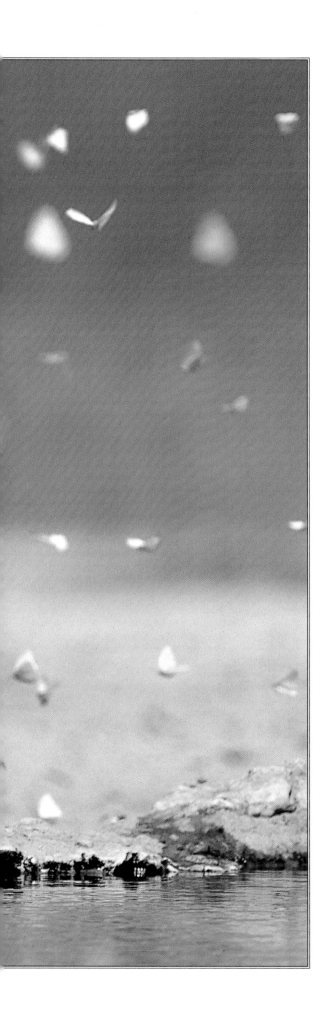

CONTENTS

ACKNOWLEDGMENTS

I would like to thank the National Parks Board for their kind support and help during the two years that I worked on this project. The following staff, researchers and friends gave invaluable assistance which ensured that my many visits to the Kalahari were not only productive but also immensely enjoyable: Keith Begg, Hendrik Bezuidenhout, Professor Tim Clutton Brock and the Nossob Suricate Research Team, Piet Cloete, Dries and Henriette Engelbrecht, Ken Erler, Piet Heymen, Pieter Kroon, Giel and Emmerentia de Kock, Klaas Kruiper, Mike Kroeger, Dawid Matthys, Dawid Pearson, Hannes Steenkamp, Daleen Ras, Lynne and Phillip Richardson, Les Lee and Malcolm Robinson, John Titus, Bertus Vilander, Dawie and Alta de Villiers, Tinnie and Lettie Visser, Isak van Wyk, Colleen Zank and all other staff of the Kalahari Gemsbok National Park.

Special thanks to Pippa Parker and her team at Struik Publishers for their tireless devotion in seeing this project to fruition. Also heartfelt gratitude to the authors Mike Knight and Peter Joyce for their meticulous attention to detail and long hours spent labouring over the text. Thanks to Geoff Wardropper and his staff at Terry's Photoworld, Pietermaritzburg, for superb film processing and always friendly and professional service and my sincere appreciation to Jane Christie for taking care of the office while I was away.

Lastly, I am immensely grateful to my wife, Wendy, for her companionship on all my Kalahari trips. Our long stays in the Kalahari required enduring searing summer temperatures, freezing winter nights and a camp destroyed during a sandstorm. However, there were many joyful experiences among the wildlife of the Kalahari and it was wonderful to be able to share these with her.

NIGEL DENNIS
KWAZULU-NATAL MIDLANDS

I thank my family first and foremost for sacrificing much of their time in this undertaking, and secondly the Kalahari for sharing its diversity and excitement with me.

MICHAEL KNIGHT
KIMBERLEY

Struik Publishers (Pty) Ltd
(a member of The Struik Publishing Group (Pty) Ltd)
Cornelis Struik House
80 McKenzie Street
Cape Town 8001

Reg. No: 54/00965/07

First published in 1997

Publishing manager: Pippa Parker
Editor: Tessa Kennedy
Designer: Peter Bosman
Editorial assistant: Helena Reid
Proofreader: Annelene van der Merwe
Cartographer: Desiree Oosterberg
Reproduced by cmyk pre-press
Printed and bound by Tien Wah Press (Pte.) Ltd

ISBN 1 86872 019 5

Front cover: Meerkats sunning at burrow; **Back cover:** Cheetah; **Spine:** Poison bulb in flower; **Front flap:** Blackbreasted snake eagle;
Half-title page: Lion; **Title page:** Cheetah; **Contents page:** Springbok with butterflies; **Foreword:** Gemsbok at sunset.
Photographic credits: All photographs in this book are by Nigel Dennis except for the following:
Getaway, D. Steele/Photo Access: p. 12; Anthony Bannister/ABPL: p. 16; A.J. Stevens/Photo Access: p. 19;
HPH Photography/Photo Access: pp. 49 (top), 50; Keith Begg: p. 114 (bottom).

FOREWORD

This book comes at a most appropriate time in the conservation history of the southern Kalahari, and southern Africa as a whole. New international initiatives are moving towards the creation of a Kalahari transfrontier park or 'peace park', incorporating the Kalahari Gemsbok National Park of South Africa and the Gemsbok National Park of Botswana into a single management unit to be run for the benefit of both nations. This will hopefully stimulate the formulation of similar ventures elsewhere along our extensive international borders.

For too long the southern Kalahari and its national parks have played second fiddle to the larger, better known conservation areas like Kruger or Chobe national parks. It is in this realm that this book has a place in bringing the Kalahari with its unique features of true, undisturbed wilderness, stark environment and well-adapted wildlife to the fore. These are the very features that have led to a doubling in tourist numbers to over 30 000 visitors a year, with almost 30 per cent of them coming from foreign countries. The prospects of a unified management and marketing of the transfrontier park will offer even more exciting recreation and wilderness experiences to the burgeoning tourism industry. It will hopefully form the economic hub in an otherwise relatively poor, inaccessible region of the subcontinent.

Through its eight chapters of informative text and superb photography the intricacies of the harsh Kalahari environment are brought to the reader, exposing details from the smallest insect to the large eland, from the plant roots buried deep in the Kalahari sands to the dropping of camelthorn pods. Although each of the chapters focuses on different themes, they are creatively intertwined, furthering the idea of interrelationships between the system's very components. Although the Kalahari seems barren, it does in fact hide a diverse multitude of life forms that are superbly adapted to the harsh environment. Their story – the quest for food and water, the struggle against intense heat and bitter cold, the very web of life – is told in these pages. The book manages to capture the mood of the desert, and illuminates the nature of its wildlife, so bringing something of this fascinating land into one's home.

Dr Anthony Hall-Martin
Director: Research & Development
National Parks Board
Pretoria

THE THIRSTLANDS

THE WIDER KALAHARI IS A VAST

REGION OF SANDY SOILS, BLEAK LANDSCAPES

AND LOW RAINFALL. BUT ONLY IN THE SOUTH DOES IT

RESEMBLE A TRUE DESERT, AND EVEN HERE THE

WILDERNESS SUSTAINS A REMARKABLE

ARRAY OF LIFE FORMS.

The legend of the unicorn, it is said, was born from the oryx of Arabia, known in sub-Saharan Africa as the gemsbok. And indeed this antelope, when seen in profile, does seem to recall the fabled equine beast with its solitary horn held proudly aloft. Like the unicorn, too, it is a splendid looking animal, stately in its bearing, eye-catching in its black, grey and white markings, dangerous in its armoury. The slender, scimitar-like horns can measure an impressive 100 centimetres (39 inches) and more from base to needle-sharp tip, and they have been known to impale lions and keep marauding hyaenas at bay.

The gemsbok is superbly adapted to desert conditions, able to live happily for months on end without drinking water: it gets its moisture from the plants that, somehow, manage to survive and, here and there, even luxuriate on the sun-blasted, formidably inhospitable terrain. For an animal of its size, too – adult bulls weigh in at a

Top *The cheetah, among the most beautiful, and vulnerable, of mammals.*
Left *Yellowbilled hornbill and prey – a Bibron's gecko.*
Right *A dust-storm sweeps its violent way through the Nossob valley.*

THE KALAHARI SANDS

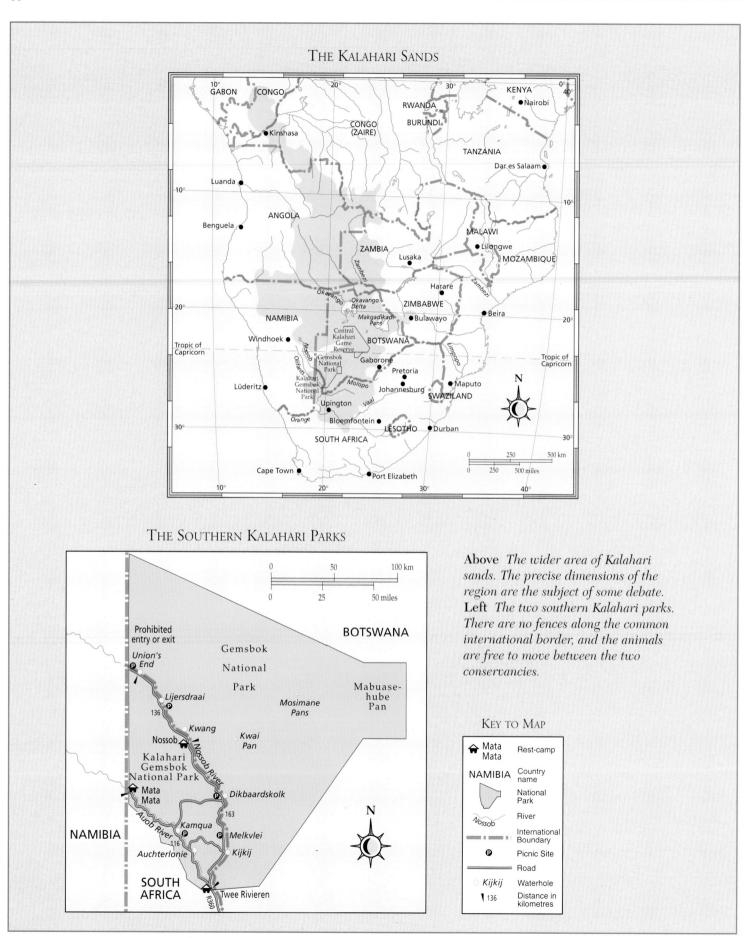

THE SOUTHERN KALAHARI PARKS

Above *The wider area of Kalahari sands. The precise dimensions of the region are the subject of some debate.* **Left** *The two southern Kalahari parks. There are no fences along the common international border, and the animals are free to move between the two conservancies.*

KEY TO MAP

Mata Mata	Rest-camp	
NAMIBIA	Country name	
	National Park	
Nossob	River	
	International Boundary	
ⓟ	Picnic Site	
	Road	
Kijkij	Waterhole	
❚ 136	Distance in kilometres	

healthy 240 kilograms (529 pounds) – it has an unusually low metabolic rate, which lessens its need for food and water. The animal's physiology and behavioural patterns are geared to the conservation of energy and fluids. It avoids the heat of the day, lying up in the shade or, in places where there are no trees, so positioning itself that the smallest possible area of its body is presented to the sun. On especially torrid days its temperature rises a few degrees above normal so that it doesn't waste precious water panting – and it then gradually re-radiates the stored-up heat during the chilly hours of the night. Its muzzle contains an intricate network of vessels in which the blood is cooled by the moisture of its nasal passages, a mechanism that protects a key part of the brain from what could otherwise be the lethally high desert temperatures.

In a word, the gemsbok is marvellously in tune with its Kalahari environment. So too are the other animals, and the plants, that inhabit these forbidding spaces. Many have evolved, each in its unique fashion, equally ingenious adaptations to the harsh conditions – the extremes of heat and cold, the lack of surface water, the scarcity of food – and, together, they have created coherent habitats in which the cycle of life, fragile and miraculous, is maintained through collective dependence.

The wider Kalahari is a vast region that stretches from South Africa's Orange River northwards, across eastern Namibia, Botswana, western Zimbabwe and into Angola, Zambia and Congo (Zaire) – a total area of more than 2,5 million square kilometres (0,97 million miles^2) , or ten times the size of Great Britain. It is commonly termed a desert because of its sandy, porous soils, its blistering summers, its far and often featureless landscapes, its low and unpredictable rainfall and its almost total lack of surface water. But only in a few places does it match the popular images conjured by the word, and is more properly defined as 'wilderness', 'thirstland' and, rather more technically, 'semi-arid biome'.

For the most part – and for most of the time – the Kalahari's broad plains are

Right *A lone gemsbok ambles across the crest of a vegetated dune near the Auob River valley in the southern park.*

mantled by a thin coat of grasses and by swathes of savanna and thorn scrub. In those areas where underground water lies fairly close to the surface, and especially when the rare rains fall, the countryside resembles parkland. Indeed, in a few areas the Kalahari is graced by an almost tropical lushness, a fertility conferred by the relatively generous rains of the northern parts and the rivers that flow down from the uplands of Angola. Prominent among these is the Kwando, which twice changes its name – first to Linyanti and then to Chobe – as it loops northeastwards to join the mighty Zambezi 70 kilometres (44 miles) upstream from the Victoria Falls, and whose reaches are magical in their moist luxuriance. Even more notable is the Okavango, a major watercourse that flows across Namibia's Caprivi 'Strip' into northwestern Botswana, where it runs

through a narrow, 100-kilometre (62-mile) long panhandle to fan out over the Kalahari sandveld in a magnificent wetland delta famed for its life-giving lagoons and labyrinthine channels, its papyrus beds, palm-fringed islands, riverine forests and richly endowed floodplains. These swamplands, however, are the striking exception in an otherwise very dry region.

To the west and southwest are the sandy wastelands of eastern Namibia (beyond whose central plateau lie the gigantic dunes of the Namib Desert and the craggy Kaokoveld). To the west, and once linked firmly to the Okavango system, are two of the world's largest saline pans, segments of the Makgadikgadi complex of vast depressions that, millennia ago, were part of an inland sea the size of and perhaps even bigger than East Africa's Lake Victoria. In those ancient times the well-vegetated

countryside sustained a wondrous array of wildlife, but it is thought that seismic disturbances reduced the flow of the northern rivers (and redirected the Zambezi River away from the central basin) to create this wilderness of salt and clay.

When the brief rains come the Makgadikgadi basin is transformed: the depressions are covered by thin sheets of water and flamingos, pelicans, waders and all manner of other waterfowl arrive in their tens of thousands (one sighting is said to have encompassed a remarkable million and more birds). The short-lived 'lakes' also attract game animals, notably herds of wildebeest, zebra and red hartebeest, from

Below *The dry reaches of the Auob River. This watercourse flows, on average, once in a decade.*

the waterless plains. But for most of the year the pans – Ntwetwe, Sowa, the smaller Nxai and Lake Mopipi – are barren, blindingly white in the searing African sun, their lifeless surfaces deceptively animated by a myriad mirages that shimmer and dance in the burning air.

To the south are the sun-baked plains of central Botswana, endless expanses of level, visually monotonous countryside. Here again, though, the bleak landscapes do have their ephemeral charm. In springtime, just before the wet season, the acacias are bedecked in their yellow and white blooms, and when the rains come the crimson lilies and wild hibiscus, the acanthus, ammocharis and many other ground plants bring splashes of modest colour to the land. The blossoms are short-lived, many are infrequent; the lilies flower for less than four days, the vellozias just once every three or four years. And then, after the brief interlude, the wilderness reverts to character, displaying little more than its scanty grasses and hardy thorn trees. And as you travel farther southwards so

the ground cover becomes thinner until, eventually, you enter a region of high red dunes and ancient watercourses, a 'true' desert that extends across the invariably bone-dry Auob and Nossob rivers and into the Gordonia region of South Africa.

Above *Vlei lilies grace the southern dunelands after the first rains fall.*
Below *A glossy starling takes advantage of one of the desert's infrequent downpours.*

The Botswana section of this immense, parched-looking and sometimes hauntingly beautiful thirstland is home to the Bushman or San people (see further on) and to small groups known as the Kgalagadi (the word from which Kalahari is derived), who arrived in the better watered eastern parts of the region about 800 years ago, bringing with them their livestock, subsistence agriculture and knowledge of metals. By the mid-19th century they had penetrated westwards, and have since lived in scattered, for the most part impoverished, desert communities surviving on the creatures they hunted, on wild plants, on the modest crops of sorghum and beans they cultivated and the few goats they kept.

The Tswana people, who comprise the majority of the wider region's inhabitants, began to appear in numbers from the latter part of the 18th century, also occupying the Kalahari's eastern fringes before fanning out to establish vast cattle ranges in the grasslands of the north-central and northern parts of what is today Botswana.

Later on, and farther south, came small groups of other peoples – Ndebele, Boer, Nama and Baster herders who preferred the hardships of isolation to life under Cape colonial rule. The Basters, mixed-descent folk of Bushman, Korana, European and slave origin, trekked into the remotest parts of the southern Kalahari to form the nucleus of what became the Mier community. Other pastoralists penetrated even deeper into the sand country.

More clearly associated with the desert, though, are the Bushmen (also referred to as San, Khoisan and, occasionally, as Basarwa and Quena), the earliest inhabitants of southern Africa.

THE BEAUTIFUL PEOPLE

Small bands of Bushman hunter-gatherers occupied the subcontinent's great sunlit spaces long before the arrival of either the Iron Age Bantu-speaking migrants from the north or the much later appearance of European colonists on the far southern seaboard. Up to some 3 000 years ago they were the dominant presence in a vast region that extended from the Atlantic to the Indian Ocean and from South Africa's Cape to parts of East Africa.

Not that the word 'dominant' is appropriate in this context: it implies a concept of authority, imposed over rivals for power and access to resources, that was entirely foreign to these gentle people. They knew nothing of competition and of the greed and malice that usually accompanies it, but instead believed, profoundly, in the need to share and cooperate – within the family, between clan and clan, between man and the environment. Custom, conviction and the dictates of survival excluded personal hostility. Nature, both animate and inanimate, was sanctified, hallowed in the mystic rituals of the hunt and the entranced dance, and in the rock paintings that embellish more than 4 000 sites throughout the subcontinent. These 'galleries' are the most visible and enduring legacy of a culture that has all but disappeared. The Bushmen, arguably the finest of all pre-historic artists, used sophisticated fore-shortening techniques and striking colours (fashioned from the mineral oxides of the earth) that gave vibrant reality to their subjects, and most notably to the hunt and the animals of the veld. Today the vitality is still there, seen in the leap of an antelope, the surge of a buffalo, and it brings bright animation to the dimness of many a long-abandoned cave.

Quite when and why the Bushmen were eliminated from all but the least hospitable regions of southern Africa have not been conclusively established, though the broad picture is clear enough. Early in the first millennium more technologically advanced black peoples from the north, who used iron, kept livestock and were territorially conscious, began to encroach on the ancient hunting grounds. Inevitably, there was confrontation, and conflict. Some of the Bushman groups were defeated and destroyed by the more warlike, better organised and better equipped immigrants; others were absorbed into the Bantu-speaking societies (who incorporated, among other things, the Bushman 'click' sounds into the Nguni and, to a lesser extent, Tswana languages).

Less speculative and wholly tragic was the fate of the southern clans – those who came into contact with the early white settlement at the Cape: their members were declared 'vermin' and hunted to death. To the Bushmen, ownership of property was an incomprehensible notion; cattle were perceived as game, to be killed and eaten. And of course they raided the herds, provoking brutal retaliation that sometimes erupted into open warfare in which the guns and horses of the settlers usually prevailed (though the protagonists were often evenly matched: the Bushmen fought with skill and courage). It appears from some of the records that up to 200 000 Bushmen might have been killed during the first two centuries of white occupation. In the remoter, more desolate parts of the subcontinent, however – in what is now the Northern Cape, Botswana and Namibia – the Bushmen remained relatively immune to both the territorial aggressiveness of the black peoples and the predations of the colonial whites.

Previous pages *The Auob valley after a storm; the pools dry out within hours.*
Opposite *A traditional Bushman hunter, bow and poison-tipped arrow at the ready, closes in on his quarry.*
Right *The African wild cat, direct ancestor of the domestic animal.*

Until very recently the desert Bushmen followed the nomadic ways of their fore-fathers, ranging at will across the sandy plains in small groups, their routines pre-scribed by the seasons, the availability of water and the movement of animals. They were hunter-gatherers (though not exclu-sively so – to a greater or lesser degree all were in contact with pastoral peoples from about AD 500, trading skins and other game products for iron, copper, salt).

For the most part it was the women who harvested the wild plants of the veld, of which 300 or so are known to be edible. The men hunted: they were superb track-ers, keen of eye and hearing (attributes born of lifelong practice rather than any special sensory endowment) and with an uncanny ability to establish direction that

Opposite, above *The tsamma melon, perhaps the most valuable of the desert's plants, is both food and drink to the animals – and to man.*
Opposite, below *An ostrich displays his maleness to impress a prospective mate.*
Right *A Bushman plays a traditional musical stringed instrument. The old ways, though, are fast disappearing.*

amounted almost to a sixth sense. Hunting tools were simple but effective: wooden bows strung with sinew; arrows carried in quivers made from bark or skin; arrowheads smeared with poison extracted from snakes, scorpions, certain plants or, most often, from the leaf-cutting beetle *Diamphidia simplex*. The toxins acted slowly on the prey animal's nervous system so that it had to be followed, sometimes for days, before it weakened. When the kill was finally made (usually by a small band of up to five men), the whole clan joined in the feast, eating, singing, and dancing to an aeons-old choreography around the night-time fire. The dance had profound spiritual significance, and often embraced a healing element.

Game meat, though, was neither a regular nor a frequent item in the Bushman diet. More usually the group would divide into smaller foraging parties to range far and wide across the countryside in search of less ambitious fare – the edible berries and roots of the desert, tsamma melons, snakes, lizards, insects. It is estimated that more than 90 per cent of the Bushman's water intake was drawn from plants, notably the tsamma (a type of cucumber) but also from other moisture-filled tubers and succulent roots. Other sources were the hollows of an occasional tree – a natural repository which lasted well into the dry season – and the so-called 'sip-well'. The latter amounted to little more than a damp, vegetated patch of sand from which the water was laboriously sucked through a grass-stem or reed, a process that involved fairly complicated preparation and took hours to complete. In times of drought, too, and in especially arid areas, the Bushmen would store water in ostrich eggshells, burying the caches at strategic points beneath the sandy surface for later recovery. The shells also provided the material for personal ornamentation,

animal skins for the clothing they wore – karosses, aprons, loincloths. Possessions were few, as befitted a highly mobile people: nothing was owned that could not be easily carried.

It is reckoned that the total Bushman population today numbers between 60 000 and 70 000, over half of whom live in Botswana, a third in Namibia and the remainder dispersed in South Africa, Angola and Zambia. Very few still follow the hunter-gatherer lifestyle: the realities

of the modern world have forced them into a more settled (and perhaps less dignified) existence in villages, on farms and, some of them, in areas set aside for their exclusive use. Those in Botswana's Central Kalahari Game Reserve have perhaps been the most successful in resisting outside pressures, though recently there have been moves by the Botswana authorities to relocate large numbers of its residents to areas where they can be better provided with resources.

THE DESERT PARKS

The Central Kalahari Game Reserve is one of several reserves that seek to protect the unique wilderness environment, its fauna and its flora from human encroachment and spoliation. It's a huge area – 60 000 square kilometres (23,166 miles²) in all (which makes it the world's second largest conservancy) – and, as its name suggests, it sprawls across Botswana's central parts. The place is home to scattered groups of Bushman people (see earlier), but also to large numbers of game animals that, because they are so remarkably well adapted, manage to thrive in a region where rainfall is rare and where there are no rivers or permanent waterholes. The area is remote, visitor facilities rudimentary. More accessible is the Khutse Game Reserve, the Central Kalahari's 2 600-square kilometre (1,004-mile²) southern appendage – a place of broad sandy plains, fossil dunes, dry river-beds and, its most distinctive component, a series of seasonal pans. Most of these depressions – once part of an extensive river system – are sandy but some are clothed in coats of grass and scatters of shrubs. Until fairly recently the reserve sustained flourishing populations of migratory antelope together with their attendant carnivores – lion, cheetah and brown hyaena among them – but veterinary fences and declining water supplies have made serious inroads into the wildlife.

Much larger are the pans of the Makgadikgadi area to the northeast (the arid relic, as we have noted, of a once-great lake) and here, too, the plains game proliferates – though less and less so as poachers, 'biltong' (meat) hunters and seekers of trophies take their toll of the herds. The wildlife is especially abundant in the northern parts, on the broad, palm-studded flatlands between Ntwetwe and Nxai pans. Here there are springbok and gemsbok, blue wildebeest and Burchell's zebra, red hartebeest and, of course, the inevitable predators that such a concourse of herbivores attracts.

Part of Ntwetwe and the whole of Nxai Pan form the 6 800-square kilometre (2,626-mile²) Makgadikgadi Pans Game Reserve. The Nxai section is different in character from the rest of the wider area: it too belonged to the ancient lakes complex but the huge, shallow depression is now grassed over, the flat monotony of its plains relieved by expanses of savanna, mopane

Opposite *The camelthorn, a member of the Acacia family, is the aristocrat of the southern Kalahari.*
Above *A lioness rests in the daytime heat of the Nossob valley.*
Right *Two young meerkats, or suricates, indulge in 'play-fighting'.*

woodland and thickets of acacia. Its wildlife complement, similar to that found further south, is enhanced by the presence of giraffe (groups of 50 can sometimes be observed) and, just after the rains, by small numbers of elephant from the wetter northern region. Nxai's birdlife embraces a surprising 250 and more different species; at certain times of the year the raptors are especially noteworthy.

Much of the Kalahari wetlands to the northwest – Okavango's delta, the flood-plains of the Linyanti and Chobe rivers

and the lush countryside of Namibia's Caprivi region – are conserved within protected areas. The Moremi Wildlife Reserve and Chobe National Park are especially renowned for their rich fauna and flora and for the magic of their watery wildernesses. But these are not part of the classic desert environment (though in winter the central and southern Chobe are arid enough) and thus fall outside the scope of this volume. Nor are the westward extensions of the sandveld and those to the northeast, which stretch across the Botswana border into Zimbabwe's famed Hwange National Park.

More typical of the Kalahari's drier regions are those that straddle Botswana's southern frontier. This is a fairly distinct ecological unit, or ecosystem. Extending for almost 500 kilometres (311 miles) from Kange, in southeastern Botswana, to a point near Gobabis in Namibia is a modest ridge which cannot be discerned by the naked eye but which is nevertheless an important physical feature. Known as the

Left and above *Rains bring life to the desert landscapes, and sustenance to the migratory wildebeest and their calves. The southern park's permanent wildebeest population numbers about 600; migrations of up to 170 000 animals occasionally occur.*

Left *Scatters of hardy vegetation help stabilize the sands of the southern dunes.* **Above** *A pair of white storks strut the Kalahari sandveld. These birds, and the more numerous Abdim's storks, are usually present only during the wet periods.* **Opposite** *Young bat-eared foxes play together near their den. Beetle larvae and harvester termites are the food favoured by these endearing little carnivores.*

Bakalahari Schwelle, it serves as a watershed, dividing the region into two large drainage basins – though the ancient rivers that drain from the ridge are invariably dry and disappear, as abruptly as they begin, in the vastness of the Kalahari sands.

The region to the south of the Schwelle embraces two enormous expanses of protected terrain: the Gemsbok National Park on the Botswana side, and South Africa's smaller Kalahari Gemsbok National Park. Together the two, plus the 'management areas' surrounding the Botswana section, comprise some 80 000 square kilometres (30,888 miles²) of protected terrain, an area about three times the size of Lesotho and somewhat larger than the Republic of Ireland. There are no fences separating them, and game are able to follow their time-honoured migratory routes, sometimes en masse – an unforgettable spectacle. The two parks (and especially the latter), their harsh landscapes, their animals and plants, provide the focus of this book.

This is a land of broad, sun-baked grassland spaces, of high red dunes, saltpans and ancient watercourses, most prominent of which are the Auob and the Nossob. The latter demarcates the border between the two countries; neither conforms to the layman's perception of a river – their beds are invariably bone-dry; the Nossob flows about once every hundred years – but there is moisture beneath the ground and nutritious minerals in the soil, and these nurture a relatively profuse plant life that includes camelthorn, blackthorn and other acacia trees, and annual grasses and herbs.

These grass- and dunelands were once the sole preserve of the ≠Khomani Bushman linguistic group but then, from about the mid-19th century, the area was penetrated by outsiders. Tswana and

Nama filtered into the wider region, and adventurous Europeans came to explore, among them William Campbell and David Livingstone, Chapman, Gordon and many others – including the eccentric and controversial G.A. Farini.

To digress for a moment: over the past century and more the reading public has been intrigued, and travellers beguiled, by tales of the 'Lost City' of the Kalahari, and numerous expeditions – about 50 in all – have set out in search of this fabulous place. The story originated with Farini, a

noted showman and acrobat (he once crossed the Niagara Falls on a tightrope), whose real name was William Leonard Hunt and who, in 1885, travelled from Cape Town to (he alleged) Lake Ngami – near the Makgadikgadi Pan system in north-central Botswana – with his son Lulu. Arriving back in Europe the following year he reported that they had found 'the ruins of quite an extensive structure' on the upper reaches of the Nossob east of the Kij Kij 'mountains'. He went on to paint a detailed picture of the ruins,

describing a wall of flat-sided stones in the shape of a mile-long arc and, on 'digging down nearly in the middle of the arc, we came upon a pavement about twenty feet wide, made of large stones . . . This pavement was intersected by another similar one at right angles, forming a Maltese cross, in the centre of which at one time must have stood an altar, column, or some sort of monument, for the base was quite distinct, composed of loose piles of fluted masonry . . .'.

Farini's account, published in book form, and his address to the Royal Geographical Society in London, caused a minor sensation at the time, but public interest soon waned. His story was hard to believe; he had produced no firm evidence (his son Lulu was an experienced photographer, but no pictures were forthcoming); there were technical and logistical discrepancies in his recollections, and some doubt that he even made the journey at all. He almost certainly did not get as far as Ngamiland. Moreover, the resources that would have been required by such a city – building materials, water, productive soils – simply do not exist in the Kalahari dunelands. In the 1920s, however, an imaginative South African academic, Prof. E.H.L. Schwarz of Rhodes University, resurrected the myth, gave it some sort of credibility, and inaugurated the era of the

exploratory expeditions. Many have been remarkable for the courage and resourcefulness of those who set out across the wilderness. All have proved fruitless.

The Farini affair, though, is a minor episode, a frivolous interlude in the saga of the Kalahari. More significant are the early white hunters who were drawn by the richness of the game, by the wildebeest and red hartebeest and, especially, by the now-unimaginable numbers of springbok, which periodically trekked en masse. Two 19th-century eyewitnesses, a medical doctor and his companion, attempted to quantify a passing parade of these graceful antelope, calculating that the trek they observed covered at least 4 000 hectares (15 miles²) of northern Cape countryside and that each hectare contained about 20 000 animals so that, by their reckoning, there were 80 million closely packed animals within their sight! This was clearly a gross exaggeration, but the concourse they observed was undoubtedly huge. Another observer reported a trek that stretched for 210 kilometres (131 miles) on a

Right and below *Twilight in the Nossob River valley – the hour when the spotted hyaena becomes active, preparing itself for the night's hunt. The Kalahari is home to two species of hyaena.*

22-kilometre (14-mile) front. The springbok no longer move across the veld in such fashion: their great migrations were a response to sudden increases in population, and the herds were decimated before the turn of the century – by settler guns, by the great rinderpest epidemic of the 1890s, and by stockfarming fences.

Following the hunters came the trekfarmers and traders who plied their oxwagons along the dry, flat river-beds, hardy men who nurtured the rare watering holes,

shot for the pot and survived well enough in the wilderness. Nevertheless, what is now the Kalahari Gemsbok National Park remained outside the colonial borders, a perceived wasteland of little economic or political account, even during the 'scramble for Africa' among the predatory big powers of Europe. Until 1897.

In that year the Cape Colony formally incorporated the territory and laid out enormous farms that were initially offered to white settlers and later, when few accepted the formidable challenge, to more intrepid coloured families. Their spacious spreads, among them Kameelsleep, Kij Kij, Twee Rivieren and others, are long gone but still remembered in the names of some of the park's waterholes (others – Dalkeith, Montrose, Craig Lockhart, Monro, Auchterlonie – reflect the Scottish origins of one Roger Jackson, who completed the area's first land survey). These early livestock farmers led a hard life on the unforgiving land: their first homes were built of sticks or wattle-and-mud (known locally as *hartbeeshuisies*), their routines governed by the shifting availability of water, tsamma melons and the widely scattered patches of short-lived grazing. They kept cattle and, initially, wool-sheep, but the all-pervading sand lowered the quality of the wool and, much later (in 1934, when an illegal shipment arrived from next-door South West Africa), they turned to karakul, the sheep that yields the fine astrakhan lamb's wool.

Meanwhile, international politics had begun to play their unwelcome part. For a brief period the area, then known as Mier Settlement, was annexed to British Bechuanaland. Numbers of Nama refugees from German atrocity in neighbouring South West Africa (now Namibia) had made their way into the area, and in 1904 German colonial troops were despatched to seal the Nossob watering places and to set up a heliograph station. Exactly a decade later, at the start of the First World War (by which time the region had been incorpo-

rated into South Africa), Louis Botha's Union government, planning an invasion route into German territory and needing a reliable source of water for its forces, sank the boreholes that were to play such an important part in the development of the future park. With the cessation of hostilities the human presence became a lot more significant, in terms of both numbers and environmental impact: hunters arrived from the south; 'borehole watchers' were appointed to keep an eye on the installations; the stockfarming community grew;

all were obliged to live off the land, and guns and ammunition were plentiful in that soldierly era. Inevitably the game populations suffered: by the 1920s several species were approaching the edge of regional extinction.

The South African government eventually responded to what amounted to an ecological crisis and in 1931, after some intensive lobbying by minister of lands Piet Grobler (who saw the light after returning empty-handed from a hunting trip along the Nossob), the Kalahari Gemsbok

National Park was formally proclaimed over the area between the Auob and Nossob rivers. Three years later more land was incorporated, establishing the boundaries we know today. In 1938 a 40-kilometre (25-mile) strip along the Bechuanaland (now Botswana) side of the Nossob was set aside as what was to become the Gemsbok National Park. The latter was initially placed under South African National Parks Board management and then – in 1972 – extended to cover a further 26 600 square kilometres (10,270 miles²), with much of the surrounding countryside designated as wildlife management areas (from which ranchers have been excluded but where controlled hunting is permitted).

Opposite *Springbok on the grassland plains. These graceful antelope are able to regulate their lambing periods to capitalize on favourable conditions.*
Below *A lone cheetah cub; offspring remain dependent for about 18 months.*

For the South African park's first rangers, Johannes le Riche and his scout Gert Jannewarie, the early years proved hard and ultimately tragic. Funds were grievously short (Le Riche earned a meagre R15 (US $3,35) a month) and the task monumental: equipped with a rifle or two, a single donkey cart and a few horses, they were expected to establish and maintain order in a huge and virtually lawless frontier area, monitor the game, and keep hunters and poachers off the land during three years of serious drought that hampered their mobility. When the rains did come at last, in 1934, they should have brought welcome relief, but the rare abundance – the Nossob flooded for the first time during the century – also created an explosive plague of mosquitoes. Both men died of malaria, and Le Riche's brother Joep took over the management of the park.

The Le Riche dynasty spanned a full six decades, Joep occupying the saddle (literally in the early days, though the park's first patrol vehicle had made its appearance in 1934) for 36 years, his sons Stoffel and

then Elias maintaining the family connection until Elias's retirement in 1995. The anti-poaching duties were initially carried out with the help of the police garrison at Tsabong, across the border in what was then still known as the Bechuanaland Protectorate. For some years both policemen and rangers patrolled on camels, exotic animals which nevertheless took readily to the Kalahari and, indeed, proved more effective – quicker over the sands, less dependent on water – than horses. Today the poachers are a lot better equipped, armed and organized than they were, and so are the patrols. Powerful four-wheel-drives and light aircraft play a major role in the protection and conservation of the region's wildlife heritage.

Originally it was intended that the park should serve as a refuge for the area's ≠Khomani Bushman inhabitants as well as for the wildlife, and indeed, despite some friction, the clan did remain to wander and hunt in the great sunlit spaces until the 1970s, when they left to live in the adjacent Mier Settlement. Many of its

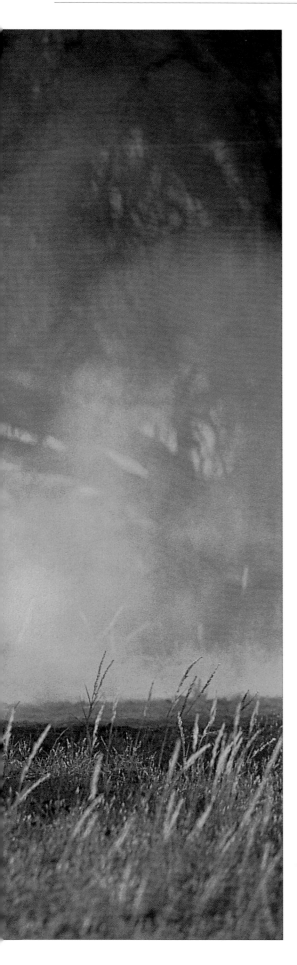

members had worked for the park's management, and some still do, applying their veld-skills to the business of tracking and to the myriad other tasks involved in game management. In the mid-1990s their leaders initiated moves to recover, through the courts, the land they had once called their own – a territory that covers about half the Kalahari Gemsbok National Park.

The first visitor facilities, three simple rondavels at the confluence of the Auob and Nossob (the camp was named Twee Rivieren, which means 'two rivers'), made their appearance in 1940, but progress on the tourism front was slow: by the mid-1950s the park was still hosting fewer than 600 people each year. Since then two more camps have been established, Mata Mata on the Auob adjacent to the Namibian border to the west, and Nossob, near the Botswana frontier. And the amenities are a lot more sophisticated. The neat, comfortable chalets are fully equipped; Twee Rivieren's are air-conditioned, and the camp has a swimming pool, a restaurant, a *lapa* for alfresco dining, and a bitumen-surfaced landing strip. Game-viewing roads, which follow the river courses, are well maintained; picnic spots have been laid out; wind- and solar-powered boreholes tap underground sources, and the dams and waterholes attract a splendid array of animals. By contrast, Botswana's adjoining Gemsbok National Park remains relatively undeveloped.

Today, around 30 000 visitors a year make their way to the Kalahari Gemsbok Park, but the authorities are highly conscious of the need to limit the numbers, to control development, and to maintain the migratory routes. The environment is too fragile to cope with much more human pressure, and will certainly not survive the introduction of fences along the common national border. Says leading research biologist Gus Mills: 'Any barrier to the movement of animals across the Nossob River will be the death-knell of the southern Kalahari ecosystem – the last more or less intact terrestrial ecosystem in southern Africa.'

Left *Rapier-horned gemsbok males fight for dominance. Most confrontations are head-on and can be lethal; the neck-hold seen here is unusual.*

Not that such a barrier is now likely to appear. The shared border has profound significance in the context of environmental management. It was realized, even in the early days, that the South African park would have to remain an integral part of the wider southern Kalahari ecosystem if it was to retain its unique character. Admittedly human interference, though kept to a minimum, has had its impact: the introduction of artificial waterholes and a southern game fence, for example, has encouraged an increase in game numbers and altered the movement patterns of the larger herbivores. Nevertheless, the system still functions naturally, allowing the game to roam freely in search of food.

This cooperation between Botswana and South Africa – sustained even during the most troubled of the apartheid years – has been the keynote, and it has laid the foundations for the subcontinent's first transfrontier or 'peace' park.

The concept of transfrontier parks – channels through which conservation ideals and practices can be carried across international borders, and which foster neighbourly relations – has been debated in world councils for some time. Such an arrangement for the southern Kalahari was proposed in 1990 (formal approval was scheduled for 1996), and will establish a joint authority to run the two parks as a single unit empowered to control the watering points, the tourist camps and infrastructure and to oversee the conservation of important and rare species. In broader terms the move should maintain the integrity of an area large enough to encompass two processes that were once a universal feature of Africa's grasslands and savannas: the large-scale migrations and nomadic wanderings of wild ungulates, and the uninhibited activities of such large carnivores as lions, leopards, hyaenas and wild dogs. On the human side it will also create employment and inject more money into the regional economy, benefits that should ensure those most vital of elements, the approval and constructive engagement of the local communities. The venture, if successful, could also have more far-reaching consequences, serving perhaps as a model for a combined mega-park embracing the giant Kruger conservancy and its lowveld neighbours in Mozambique and Zimbabwe.

FAR HORIZONS

DROUGHT IS THE NORMAL CONDITION IN THE

SOUTHERN KALAHARI. FOR MOST OF THE TIME THE LAND LIES

COMATOSE UNDER THE SCORCHING AFRICAN SUN, ITS PLANTS

WITHERED, ITS ANIMALS HIDDEN, SEEKING WHAT LITTLE SHADE

THEY CAN FIND. BUT WHEN THE RARE RAINS COME, THE

COUNTRYSIDE BECOMES A PARKLAND PARADISE.

About a dozen times during the blazing Kalahari summer a strong morning breeze blows in from the north, bringing rare and welcome rain to the parched land. By early afternoon the breeze has become a wind that lifts, sweeps and swirls the loose sand high into the air, obscuring vision, stinging the flesh and darkening the sky. Overhead the clouds are building up, massive banks of moisture-laden cumulonimbus angry with the rumble of thunder and the flash of lightning. And then comes the rain – a deluge that is fierce in its gift and lasts perhaps half an hour – to rejuvenate the tired earth, to green the wilted grasslands and lift the jaded human spirit. For a brief while all is bright, fresh, new.

The southern Kalahari does not experience the traditional calendar seasons. Summer and winter merge into each other, spring and autumn last no more

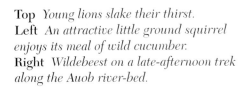

Top *Young lions slake their thirst.*
Left *An attractive little ground squirrel enjoys its meal of wild cucumber.*
Right *Wildebeest on a late-afternoon trek along the Auob river-bed.*

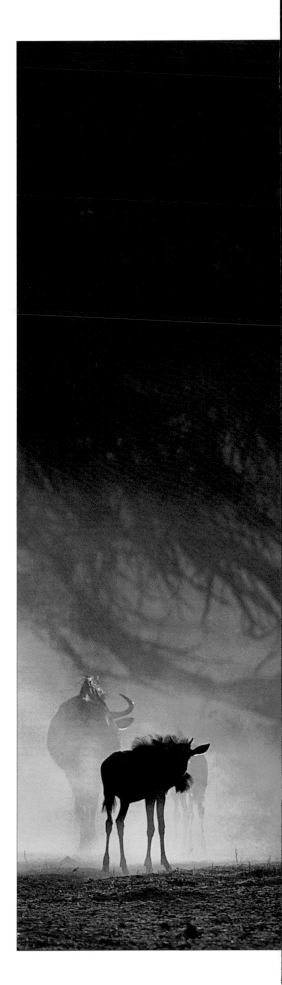

Left *Wind-driven dust shrouds a solitary gemsbok. The signs are propitious; rain could be on the way.*
Above *After the deluge – short-lived pools moisten, and bring sudden life to the normally bone-dry river-bed.*

than a few days; one or two plants, like the camelthorn and blackthorn, put on a modest display of spring flowers but most wait it out until the rains come. The true seasons are better defined in other terms, by temperature and rainfall: cold-dry, hot-dry and hot-wet.

The wet season, such as it is, usually runs from the end of October through to March, sometimes April, but the rains are patchy, unreliable and unpredictable, and because the deep sands will absorb and the fierce African sun will quickly evaporate everything the heavens can deliver, none

of the life-giving water remains on the surface for very long. In that sense, the Kalahari is a true desert.

The actual amount of rain received varies prodigiously from place to place. Generally, though, the farther north the area the wetter the climate. Northeastern Botswana (which enjoys a healthy mean of around 650 millimetres, 26 inches, a year) gets more than the southwestern wilderness, some parts of which average 250 millimetres (10 inches), others even less; the

dune area's mean is 150 millimetres (6 inches); the Nossob camp received just 50 (2 inches) in 1994. This has nothing to do with the nature of the terrain, everything to do with latitude, high atmospheric pressure and the blocking effect of the great Drakensberg rampart flanking the Indian Ocean in the east. Moreover, there are sharp differences within relatively small areas: one of the Kalahari Gemsbok Park's rest-camps, for instance, might be blessed by regular deluges in February and March (normally the wettest months of the year) while another will suffer virtually unrelieved drought.

This patchiness plays a significant role on the ecological stage, creating a kind of feast-and-famine scenario in which isolated areas are suddenly transformed into green islands that briefly flourish in an ocean of sand and sun-scorched grass. Birds and the larger mammals, those that are able to move fair distances across the land, can follow where the rain leads to feed on the nutritious new growth. Other fauna, smaller and less mobile, stay in their home ranges, awaiting their turn for the blessing of rain. This may be months in the future, perhaps years. But they are well adapted to the unpredictability, and the chances are that their patience will eventually be rewarded.

The region is also subject to extremes of temperature. On summer days the thermometer rarely sinks below 30 °C (86 °F), and often breaches the 40 ° (104 °F) mark. And that's just the heat of the air; at ground level it can be a searing 70 °C (158 °F) and more. Because there is no cloud cover and little vegetation, though, the atmosphere, and to a lesser extent the ground, rapidly cools as darkness sets in. Winter days are hot, the brilliantly starred nights and early mornings bitterly cold, temperatures sometimes dropping to a bone-chilling -14 °C (20 °F).

THE MAKING OF A DESERT

Temperature is affected to some extent by altitude. Most of the Kalahari lies more than 1 000 metres (3,280 feet) above sea level, and is part of the Great African Plateau that rises in the Sahara Desert some 4 000 kilometres (2,500 miles) to the north. But that is about all the two deserts have in common: they are separated by the great tropical forests of the continent's central regions, and the Kalahari has its own, very distinctive origins, history and

personality. It is, above all, a product of aeons of geophysical change – of gigantic seismic convulsions, of other massive forces that shifted and warped the land, and of a climate that seesawed between extreme dryness and tropical luxuriance.

In the age of the dinosaurs, during the Triassic period some 230 million years ago, the supercontinent of Gondwanaland – parent body to Antarctica, South America, Africa, Madagascar, India, Australia and New Zealand – consisted almost entirely of vast, wind-blown expanses of desert-like terrain that nevertheless managed to sustain a surprisingly prolific plant and animal life. The region occupied by today's Kalahari was especially arid: it lay at the continental centre, separated from the rain-producing oceans by what was to become South America in the west and by the future India and Australia in the east, and its surface was relentlessly eroded, and redeposited, by the elements to create the Karoo sediments we know today. (These fossil-rich deposits are an especially happy hunting ground for modern palaeontologists and also provided the myriad caves that sheltered the early Bushmen.)

About 30 million years later the scene began to change. The earth's crust split, opening fissures from which great outpourings of basalt lava emerged to mantle the surface of Gondwanaland. The process lasted about 70 million years, during which the supercontinent gradually fractured to produce its various offspring and, with infinite slowness, nascent Africa moved a little southwards into new climatic zones while other landmasses drifted farther afield. When the lava finally stopped flowing two different forces came into play: on the one hand wind and water erosion began to

Above *The normally drab driedoring (soapbush) plants of the Kalahari come briefly, and enchantingly, into flower after a good downpour.*
Right *Harvest of the desert: the gemsbok cucumber is a sustaining source of food for many desert animals.*

level the terrain, filling the great depressions with clays, gravels and later with sand while, on the other, periodic volcanic action thrust up the ridges (or dykes) and rocky outcrops (sills) that today relieve the

flat, otherwise featureless monotony of the Karoo. The deserts returned again, high winds filling the basins and river valleys with great quantities of sand and gravel and, from about 65 million years ago (the Tertiary period), the Kalahari began to assume its familiar character.

The final chapter in the Kalahari's evolutionary story unfolded quite recently on the geological calendar: between 10 and 15 million years ago, Africa's topography began to be changed in infinitely slow but ultimately dramatic fashion by immensely powerful forces that are still not fully understood. It was during this period that the Great Rift Valley appeared, creating a spectacular swathe of deep canyon and high volcanic mountain down the eastern flank. In a complementary sequence the southern subcontinent sank lower in places, higher in others – the upward tilt at its most prominent around the perimeter of the landmass – to create a massive rearrangement of the region that forced many of the rivers either to change direction or lose momentum. Among the affected watercourses were those that had nurtured the Kalahari and, in partnership with the rains, had redistributed its sandy soils. These, which today comprise the earth's largest uninterrupted expanse of sand, were now permanently secured in position (or as permanently as anything can be in the realm of geophysics). Over several periods of the remote past the Kalahari was even more arid than it is today, a fact to which its ancient dunefields testify. There are many of these, great tracts of rolling sand that cover a surprisingly large part of southern and central Africa. Surprising, because these fossil systems are not immediately apparent to the casual eye (though clearly discernible from the air): most have long since been bound into permanency and disguised by the plant life of the sandveld. Not all, however, are so effectively hidden.

THE DUNELANDS

As noted, the southern parts of the Kalahari are the driest, most closely conforming to the image of a true desert. But even here the soft sand dunes have their patchy vegetation, without which they would be vulnerable to the rain and, more especially, to the wind, continually

Opposite *A typical Kalahari sand ridge, its sandy soil stabilized by a straggling mantle of hardy plants, most common of which is the long-stemmed* duineriet.
Above *A cheetah monitors its hunting ground from a dune-top vantage point.*

changing their profiles so that seeds would find it impossible to take root and flourish. They still do change, but very slowly, and they owe their comparative stability partly to a remarkably hardy and ingenious type of grass: *Stipagrostis amabilis*. This species, commonly known as *steekriet* or *duineriet* (Afrikaans for dune-reed), sends out a 'root' which in reality is a long stem bearing a full complement of buds and shoots. The stem snakes through the loose sand near or on the dune's crest, where it stops and in due course grows into a large, tough clump a metre and more in height. Sand banks up around the tuft, providing a moderately firm and shady environment for a few other plants. Most common of

those that manage to establish themselves in these unlikely spots are the brooms, whose slender shapes offer little resistance to the desert breezes. Further down, on the lower slopes, and in the dune valleys where the soil contains more clay and is more compacted, there is a more luxuriant growth of grasses, shrubs and trees.

The park embraces some irregular dune clusters, but for the most part the dune formations of the southwest, which extend for some 800 kilometres (497 miles), are curiously symmetrical, arranged in long, roughly parallel ranks which, when viewed from above, lend a strikingly ripple-like appearance to the countryside. The sand here is ochre-red (more so in the higher and drier parts), a colour conferred by the iron oxide that envelopes the grains. Elsewhere, notably in the less arid areas of the north, rain leaches away the oxide to produce a more pastel landscape.

The actual size of the grains plays an important part in the retention of moisture. Generally speaking, the coarser sands

hold more water than the finer ones because they better absorb the rain, and there is less runoff. Moreover, they are subject to weaker capillary forces, so that there is less upward movement of the water and thus less evaporation. The coarser sands cover about nine-tenths of the southern Kalahari; the finer ones are more or less restricted to the river-beds and pans. Conversely, though, the beds and pans, because they are at a lower level than the surrounding countryside, receive most of the minerals leached down by the rains. All of which creates something of an anomaly: the beds and pan-perimeters support a better quality of plant life even though their soils are generally drier.

There are also differences in the nature of the sand within the dunes themselves. That of the crests and upper slopes contains less silt, the grains are smaller and, as noted, tend to be darker than the soil in the inter-dune 'streets', factors which also affect both the type of vegetation and the character of the animal com-

munities (conditions in the lower areas, for example, favour the burrow-dwelling reptiles and rodents). There is, therefore, surprising diversity behind the monotonous face the Kalahari dune system presents to the casual observer.

Among the unique phenomena of the far southern region – and a long way from the park – are the 'roaring sands', an extraordinary, 9-kilometre (6-mile) long, 2-kilometre (1.2-mile) wide 'island' of high white dunes, known as Witsand, near the Northern Cape hamlet of Groblershoop to the southeast of Upington. The dunes rise some 100 metres (328 feet) above the otherwise flat, reddish land, and in especially dry weather the loose sand of the southern face, when disturbed (even slightly, by for instance running your hand through it), produces an eerie moaning sound that can sometimes become a muted roar. The noise has something to do with the dune's granular texture and with its composition (it comprises an unusually low ratio of fine grains), elements that prevent it mixing with the firmer red sand below. But nobody really knows for sure.

A PROFUSION OF PANS

The Makgadikgadi complex of north-central Botswana is renowned for its enormous salt- and grassland pans (see page 20), but they are by no means the Kalahari's only ones. There are uncountable numbers of these shallow depressions scattered throughout the region, each different in shape and size from the next. Some are large, most less than 5 square kilometres (1.9 mile²) in extent, their clay floors smooth, hard and very often white with brine from the action of long-evaporated rainwater. In many cases nothing grows on the surface. But to much of the Kalahari's life forms these pans are life-sustaining oases, natural drainage basins that capture and hold the water runoff during the rainy season, sometimes for a month or more. They also provide the animals with the mineral salts they need; game trails will often lead straight to a salt-lick, invariably located close to the edge of the pan. Their surrounds, too, moist for a fair part of each summer, are comparatively well endowed with plant life – saline tolerant grasses near the edges, shrubs and trees further out.

Here again, though, there appears to be no firm consensus on the physical origins of these desert features. They do tend to occur in clusters along the region's modest watersheds and seem to be the remnants of ancient riverine drainage systems. Many are flanked on their leeward sides by a brace of sand dunes, usually a larger outer and a smaller inner one, that represents two different phases of pan formation. The pans collect a great deal of loose sand and detritus. Moreover, their surfaces are trampled by game in quest of minerals, and the periodic heavy traffic reduces much of the upper clay to a fine powder that is easily blown away. Both dunes are the product of winds that carried off and heaped this surface material, but the larger is thought to date to an earlier time,

Opposite, above *A spotted hyaena curled up against the cold evening air.*
Opposite, below *Steenbok are commonly seen among the dunes.*
Right *The barren, rock-hard surface of Kwang Pan. When rain falls, however, the Kalahari's pans become life-giving oases.*

when the region was more desert-like, the sands looser and the winds stronger. The smaller dune appeared later, after the direction of the prevailing wind had veered slightly and the climatic conditions had become generally milder.

The southern dune system embraces about a thousand pans that serve as seasonal waterholes and sources of salt. They are at their most prominent in the areas to the west of the Auob river-bed, in the Schwelle, near the northeastern border of the Botswana park; and to the east and north of Union's End, on the upper reaches of the Nossob, although the wide sandy spaces between the two rivers are also well enough endowed.

TWO RIVERS

The southern Kalahari – if one discounts the mighty Orange – has no perennial rivers. Indeed no watercourses of any significance rise in the entire region. Aeons ago, in the wetter climatic periods, some scoured their way across the land, but nothing remains of their courses save their wide, now-empty and often barely discernible valleys.

Nevertheless, the southern Kalahari has its river system. The Molopo flows southeastwards through a vast, steep-sided valley – which attests to its once-eminent status – to form a substantial segment of the Botswana-South Africa border. Just

below it on the map, and running roughly parallel, is the Kuruman. Both these are fed by underground springs (the Kuruman's 'eye', near the Northern Cape town of the same name, yields an impressive 20 million litres, or 5.3 million US gallons, of sparkling water each day) but neither runs for any great distance. In fact, the Molopo hasn't flowed its full length, to its confluence with the Orange, for at least a century. Invariably, even in flood years, it comes to a halt at a spacious pan called Abiquasputs, which, in especially good seasons, is transformed from a formidably barren place of mirages and dust devils into a limpid lake that hosts fish and a splendid array of migrant birds.

Two of the Molopo's tributaries – the Auob and the Nossob – make their way down from the northwest, all four watercourses eventually joining together south of the Botswana border to set course towards the Orange. The major portion of the Kalahari Gemsbok National Park lies between these two rivers, which serve as the principal components of its ecosystem.

The Nossob valley, which meanders a lot and is fringed by oxbow lakes, is divided into two fairly distinct sections. The upper, running from the Namibian border, has a broad bed, a slightly raised alluvial floodplain and widely spaced flanking dunes, all of which creates an impression of spaciousness. However, half-way between the Twee Rivieren and Nossob camps its course suddenly cuts through calcrete deposits and turns southwestwards, and the feeling of expansive openness changes to one of confinement and concentration. Here its banks are relatively steep, narrow and rocky, and the further downriver one travels the fewer trees one sees growing in its bed. The few that do occur are, in summer, a prime attraction for game animals, as well as birds in search of refuge and roosting sites. The Auob River is similar in some respects – it also has two discernible segments – but different in appearance and atmosphere, its character conferred largely by the beautiful stands of large grey camelthorn trees that grace all but the last 30 kilometres (19 miles) of its course.

For most of the year these ancient rivers are dry, flowing only occasionally, their beds and banks holding little save the occasional twisted thorn tree, the hard, cracked remains of an old mud-wallow and the ever-encroaching sand of the dunes. The Auob, on average, runs for a reasonable distance just once every 11 years, the Nossob once or perhaps twice every hundred. They do, however, carry rainwater in the wet season, and there is moisture beneath their beds, a precious resource that is tapped by wind- and solar-pumped

boreholes. The latter are vital elements in the fight waged for survival by all the desert's larger and more mobile living forms, especially when the rains fail and everything in and beyond the river-beds withers under the scorching African sun.

In the past, when the vegetation of the southern Kalahari succumbed to sustained drought, the animals – many of which normally gain their moisture from food plants – would migrate, the herds moving across the land in quest of grazing, sometimes as far south as the Orange River. No longer. There are no artificial barriers along much of the international border – the Nossob – but electrified game-fences gird the southern, western and, a recent feature, eastern perimeters of the South African park, and a 120-kilometre (75-mile) fence was recently erected along the

Opposite *A grey camelthorn tree stands against the storm-darkened sky.*
Right *A springbok ewe. These antelope sometimes migrate across the plains in huge numbers; on one such mass trek, in 1950, the herds moved south on a front some 300 kilometres (186 miles) broad.*

southern border of the Gemsbok National Park. Another runs along Botswana's western border with Namibia, and many others criss-cross the farming areas of the Northern Cape. So the game herds are much more confined than they were, and the boreholes have proved a blessing – though they are sometimes hard put to cope with the demand.

During the great drought of 1985, for instance, a huge concourse of blue wildebeest and smaller but still substantial numbers of eland and red hartebeest trekked southwards, drawn perhaps by the scent of distant, sweet grazing. They found their progress blocked by the fences and changed course, moving restlessly and aimlessly along the Auob River in quest of water and food that simply weren't there. About 30 of the boreholes were quickly

upgraded to increase their output and these did sterling duty but, still, thousands of the animals died from starvation, first the deserted calves, whose mothers could no longer suckle them, and the old bulls who had been consigned to the poorest ground, and then the stronger but rapidly weakening young adults. Many stood listless in their final days, waiting patiently in the sun for the onset of death – a cornucopia for the predators. Carcasses littered the scorched veld; vultures swooped, settled and gorged. Some of the animals were driven off – stolen – by farmers from the south, who fattened them up for profitable sale; a few were captured and translocated to better-off conservation areas elsewhere. The survivors then moved on, eventually finding their way back by a circuitous route to the Botswana side.

THE DESERT FLORA

Compared to very dry regions like the Namib, the southern Kalahari sustains an impressive number and diversity of geophytes – bulbs, corms and tubers that are encouraged by the relatively high rainfall and stable deep soils.

Most of the area's plants – about 70 per cent in all – are 'escape-type' species that wait out the harsh, waterless periods in the form of seeds, bulbs and dormant buds which lie on the soil surface. But the perennial grasses of the park are what attracts the herds southwards: most of the grazing farther north, in the tree savanna that covers the northeastern segment of Botswana's Gemsbok National Park, comprises annual grasses that disappear in the long dry periods.

THE DESERT'S LIFE-GIVING HARVEST

Rivalling the shepherd's tree in multi-use value, though in quite different ways, are three wild plants: the tsamma melon, the gemsbok cucumber and, to a lesser degree, the wild cucumber supply both moisture and food to the animals of the desert, and to man. The tsamma (right), an annual species which ripens in midwinter (the driest period), looks rather like a small watermelon growing on a long stem. The plants make rather bland eating, and their calorific content is low, but they contain plenty of Vitamin C, some useful trace elements and, of course, precious water. The gemsbok cucumber's fruit, oval shaped with sharp spikes and yellowish green when mature, is rather smaller but has a disproportionately large, fleshy, distasteful root that penetrates a good metre and more into the sand and, despite its bitterness, is much favoured by gemsbok and mole-rats.

Antelope – gemsbok, hartebeest and eland – feed on these plants, sometimes digging down to get at the cucumber's root, chewing its fibrous pith for the moisture it contains. So too do some carnivores, among them jackals and honey badgers. Springbok, steenbok and the Kalahari's two species of hyaena relish the plants. These animals cannot absorb the seeds, which are full of protein and vegetable fat: their digestive acids merely break down the hard outer coverings, pass the rest out in their waste and so help in the seed dispersal process (see page 121). The plants are also much sought-after by squirrels, porcupines, crickets and an array of other rodents and insects. They were also a vital part of the traditional Bushman's survival regime (see page 19), *serving as caches of water and as a valuable, at times essential food source. They can be eaten raw but were usually prepared by covering them with fire – heated sand and hot ash – and leaving them to cook overnight. The seeds, when roasted or fried and ground, make a reasonably palatable flour-like substance; the round shell of the tsamma is sturdy enough to be used as a pot. Early travellers relied on these plants for sustenance. The Bushmen, apparently, could live on nothing else but these wild fruits for weeks on end although outsiders, with their pampered digestive systems, would probably not last long in the desert without dietary reinforcement.*

The perennials withstand the rainless months simply by dying back and waiting for the next downpour, surviving the ferocious heat of the ground with the help of their insulating hair-roots. Notable among them are the feathery Bushman's grasses that lend such delicate grace to the otherwise harsh countryside. Other common types include the dune-reed, so successful in stabilizing the soft red sand (*see page 39*); the ghaa- and love-grasses which also grow on the dune slopes; and the Kalahari Bushman grass (Afrikaans: *suurgras*), which grows tall and golden among the dunes and along the river-banks. The latter, though, is an annual that appears only after good rain, and its presence is not all that welcome: although the grazing animals are drawn to the tender new shoots these soon toughen, secreting an unpalatable acid substance from the hairs of the stalks and flowers (the secretion can cause skin irritation, and when you drive through it your vehicle will soon be covered in a thick, sticky black paste). Moreover, the dense, dry stands are highly vulnerable to

Opposite *A camelthorn tree provides a daytime resting place for this Cape fox, a primarily nocturnal animal.*
Below *The colourful swallowtailed bee-eater, a common resident.*

lightning-initiated fire and they blaze violently and destructively, consuming the lovely old camelthorn trees and much else. But this, like everything that happens in the wilderness, is part of the natural order, harmful in some respects perhaps, beneficial in others: among other things the conflagrations clear the veld of a suffocating mass of dead vegetation that accumulates after the rains. In the riverine areas you'll also find the perennial speckled vlei and buffalo grasses, and the annual feather-top chloris (Afrikaans: *vleigras*) and hardy bristle-burr species.

A surprising variety of shrubs, known locally as *bossies*, survive and even flourish in the wilderness. Most visible are the *driedoring* (Afrikaans for three-thorns) and the *bessiebos* or brandy bush of the dunes, which yields a fruit much favoured by jackals and most frugivores and by the distillers of an illicit, powerful home-brew known as *mampoer*. Several riverine trees, blackthorn and candle-acacia among them, grow in shrub form on the dunes, where conditions are a lot less favourable.

One species that does thrive in the dune system is the shepherd's tree or *witgat*, perhaps the area's most important food plant: its leaves are full of protein, its flowers rich in nectar, its fruits savoured by birds. The tree (of which there are in fact two types: the shepherd's and the smelly shepherd's; *(see also page 121)* is a member of the caper family, and is easily recognizable by its round shape, the branches reaching down almost to the ground to provide a welcome shade-bower for an animal – anything from a lion to a spring-hare – in retreat from the midday sun (the temperature in its shade can be 20 °C (68 °F) lower than that in the open). Its often hollow trunk, too, acts as a life-sustaining storage tank, collecting rainwater and retaining it during the long dry weeks and months. And, for man, it has other practical uses. The hard white wood is suitable for making utensils and implements, although some folk attach spiritual significance to the tree and will not cut its wood.

The leaves and fruit are said to have medicinal value: an infusion from the former is used for bovine eye infections; extracts from the latter apparently help in the treatment of epilepsy. The preserved flower-buds are reputed to rival the best of traditional capers in quality. The roots, when roasted and ground to a powder, make a very passable coffee-like beverage. They also serve as an excellent preservative, maintaining the freshness of milk and butter long after deterioration usually sets in, and keeping such food items as fruit, potatoes and bread free of mould.

Prince of the trees, though, is the ubiquitous camelthorn, a handsome, slow-maturing species with a tangled mass of branches, evergreen canopy and deeply furrowed stem that can eventually reach 15 metres (49 feet) in height in the riverine areas (it is found on the dunes, too, but there its root system is starved of moisture and the tree mostly occurs in smaller form). It can and does hybridize with its

Above *The shepherd's tree, valuable for the fodder and shade it provides.*
Opposite *Ever-watchful meerkats sunbathing near their burrow on a cool autumn morning. They also construct bolt-holes in foraging areas.*

cousin the grey camelthorn, which has silvery grey leaves and grows only along the Auob River. The camelthorn – which in fact has nothing to do with camels, deriving its name instead from the Afrikaans word for giraffe (*kameelperd*) – is really the only large southern African tree that penetrates into areas which get less than 400 millimetres (16 inches) of rain a year. After displaying its beautiful yellow blossoms in early summer, the huge, shiny, hairy pods slowly develop through and beyond the hot months to drop during the cold winter period, the time when they are most needed. The tree's leaves, flowers and pods are savoured by a great many life forms; its spreading foliage serves as home to birds, lizards and tree rats. Among other acacias present are the blackthorn (Afrikaans: *swarthaak*), a tree valuable for the browse it provides and for the flowers it produces, and the bastard umbrella thorn (Afrikaans: *swartbas*), an inhabitant of the park's northern dunes and the tree savanna of the Botswana side.

Completing the South African park's modest complement of trees are the silver terminalia cluster-leaf (Afrikaans: *geelhout*) that grows here and there on the crests of the dunes; the worm-bark falsethorn of the northern parts, whose leaves and bark are apparently an effective remedy for parasitic worms; the smelly shepherd's tree; the wild green-hair tree (Afrikaans: *lemoendoring*), and the occasional buffalo-thorn and sweetthorn. Only three of the southern Kalahari's trees, the camelthorn, the grey camelthorn and the shepherd's tree, are evergreen; the rest drop their leaves towards the end of winter to stand like emaciated sentinels in the wilderness of sand.

Beyond the dunefield to the northeast, in the Gemsbok National Park, the vegetation becomes thicker in parts, the clusters of trees and shrubs, embraced in a rain-blessed summer by seas of golden grass, taller, more numerous and diverse, interspersed with the occasional open grassland supporting scattered bushes. The earth immediately surrounding the trees, though, is often bare, the ground cover strangled by their moisture-seeking roots. Between the wooded savanna areas are plains that stretch to the far horizons, their level surfaces densely mantled in grasses and scatters of low bushes – a landscape very different from one's immediate idea of a desert. In the long dry periods, though, the scene changes, the relatively luxuriant growth replaced by short, hard, dull-brown, needle-sharp grass stubble and leafless shrubs.

THE COMING OF THE RAINS

September and October – hope-filled springtime in the gentler southern climes – are the dread months. The land, already comatose from the long winter drought, is now assaulted by rising heat, and by the desiccating breezes of the desert. Much has died since the last rains, among the

casualties those plants without storage organs and whose roots do not reach deep into the ground for what moisture is left. The annuals have long since gone; the perennial grasses are dormant, the only signs of growth the occasional pale-green blade peeping from clumps of old, brittle, sun-hardened stems and leaves.

The river-beds look exhausted, everything in them – save for the hardiest of evergreen plants – scorched to the dull-grey colour of the sand, leached of life, haggard in the blinding light. Now and then a violent little dust devil makes its drunken way across the baked terrain. The air shimmers and dances, playing tricks with your eyes, creating mirages, impressions of floating trees and pan-edges around which springbok graze. The silence is profound, absolute: most of the birds have departed for kinder parts, the game herds for greener pastures; no nocturnal creature dares venture into the daytime furnace; other animals find what shade they can and wait with quiet fatalism for the coming of a cooler twilight. And for the rain. It is ten months since this particular patch of desert last received a downpour and the long-awaited wet season is

approaching, but there is no certainty that the rains will come soon, or at all.

This year they do. The wind grows stronger, stirring the dead acacia blooms that litter the ground, sweeping drifts of sand down the slip-faces of the dunes and talcum-like dust from the river-beds, filling the sulphurous sky with a hot, choking haze, obscuring the sun. Humidity has

climbed to almost unbearable levels, and body and spirit cry out for relief.

But now there is something new in the air, that most subtle and evocative of hints that tells you that somewhere, not too far away, rain has fallen on the veld. It is a faint but magical scent – of damp earth, of life and promise – and it quickens the senses with anticipation.

The first white clouds appear over the horizon to the north. They are scattered and ineffectual, but as the day wears on they grow in size and number, darkening to a menacing blue-grey colour, rising, swelling to become massive, majestic billows that rumble and flash and flicker. The pattern is repeated the next day, and the next and the next, each accumulation of clouds raising hopes of relief before it passes on without yielding its bounty. One afternoon, however, a few cold raindrops fall, raising tiny puffs of dust from the bed of the river and quickly disappearing into

Opposite, above *Springbok and sand-grouse share space at a waterhole.*
Opposite, below Perdebos; *tough, highly adapted plants of the southern Kalahari.*
Right and below *'Devil's thorn' flowers cover the dunes after the first spring rains, lending beauty to this austere land.*

the thirsty sand. And then the heavens open, hurling down a torrent of water to create puddles and pools and rivulets, filling first the pans and beds, turning the dunes to a deeper blush of red.

Within half an hour the storm is spent: the clouds have moved away to the southeast and the sun is shining again.

Over the next few days the land takes on a new and very different personality. Life becomes frenetic, for there is so little time to emerge, to feed, reproduce, complete the cycle before the water is gone. Almost immediately the dragonflies arrive to hover in their multitudes, and the pools swarm with water-boatmen and other minute creatures – including that most ancient of living forms, the tadpole shrimp. This is one of the few terrestrial organisms that has thrived over the aeons – in this case, for close on 300 million years – without responding to the evolutionary demands imposed by changing climates

there they stay, happy in their long sleep, until the next rainfall (which could be more than a year in the future), when they re-emerge. In the interim, astonishingly, they lose little of their body weight. These amphibians, like the invertebrates, must make the very most of the brief bonanza, eating as much and as quickly as they can. The bullfrogs are especially voracious, taking anything that moves and breathes including insects, rodents, reptiles, birds, other bullfrogs and even, if you're careless in your approach, the ends of your fingers. Breeding is also a frantic process: the eggs hatch within two days of mating (competition for mates is fierce), and within 18 days the tadpoles have become frogs.

Then there are the arboreal anurans or tree frogs, whose drought-survival mechanisms – the species can resist desiccation for surprisingly long periods in the semi-desert – remain something of a mystery. Their success, though, obviously has a lot to do with their ability to locate just the right moist microclimate into which to escape, and with the waterproofing qualities of their skin, properties which minimize moisture loss (in this respect the frogs are strangely akin to the desert lizards).

The region's tortoises are also dormant in the long dry periods, finding the most sheltered place available in which to hide and reducing their physiological processes to the bare minimum. In the wet season you'll see two species: the small Kalahari tortoise, and the much bigger leopard or mountain tortoise. The former has an unusual way of drinking the rain, hunching forward, lifting its rear and licking the moisture runoff from its carapace. A related reptile and something of an oddity in the southern Kalahari is the Cape terrapin, which, like the bullfrog, buries itself in the sand for the duration of the drought and emerges with the rain.

For a few weeks after the rain the country-side is miraculously transformed, clothed in robes of tall, bright green grass that has

and habitats. The shrimp is marvellously adapted in every way to unpredictable conditions, living in the temporary rain-water pools of the world's arid areas – and, in southern Africa, in the wildlife mud-wallows, pans and waterholes that often dry out completely. It is an omnivorous species, eating anything it can find, from algae and plant detritus to other arthropods and even members of its own kind. It has remained happily in its original form, wholly untouched by the earth's great dramas, probably because it has no predators of its own: the pools last for too short a time to nurture enemies. This, though, is just one species in a vast concourse of near-invisible crustaceans that the rain awakens. Most of the tiny creatures over-winter in the form of eggs, which are highly resistant to desiccation and to the intense heat. Indeed some are able to withstand temperatures approaching boiling point! They are surprisingly mobile, too, moving between pans in the mud stuck to the feet of birds and mammals.

Frogs appear from nowhere, as if by magic, to sit around in the pools and pans and croak their evening symphony. They come in three types (five species altogether): the small sand and rain frogs, and the bulky (up to 20 centimetres, or 8 inches,

long) bullfrogs, the males of which establish territories and become violently aggressive in their hurry to feed and in their competition for mates.

One might well wonder how these apparently water-dependent amphibians, technically known as anurans, manage to survive in a region where drought is the normal condition. Again, there are three broad types of anuran, each of which has different needs and responds to environmental challenges in different ways. The aquatic ones do depend on a virtually constant availability of open water, and will migrate when the source declines below a certain level. There are none of these in the southern Kalahari. The fossorial anurans, on the other hand, although they also need moisture in order to feed and breed, can live through the rainless months by burrowing beneath the sand-and-clay surfaces of the pans and, when the soil dries up, entering into a state of dormancy, or suspended animation, known as aestivation. In this condition all but the most essential of the body organs – heart, lungs, kidneys – are shut down for the duration. The frogs also enclose themselves in a waterproof cocoon, fashioned from the outer layers of their skin, which further reduces the loss of body moisture. And

an almost lawn-like quality when seen from a distance. Trees and shrubs, their dusty coats washed away, stand clean and fresh. Doves and sandgrouse, lovebirds, coursers, larks, drongos, flycatchers, weavers, martins, starlings and a host of other birds congregate, lending joyous animation to the scene. The animals of the wider area – springbok and eland, wildebeest, gemsbok, duiker, red hartebeest, steenbok – have smelt the rain and they too begin to home in on the oasis. Their predators often follow not too far behind.

Opposite *A marsh terrapin emerges from the mud of a pan after the two-year drought is broken. Two species of tortoise also occur in the southern Kalahari.*
Above *The rewards of rain – a small herd of blue wildebeest gather to feed on the succulent young grasses of the Nossob valley.*

This is the time when the desert ephemerals put on their rare and lovely show, turning dune and river-bed into a tapestry bright with the yellow of *dubbeltjie*, the purple of cat's tail, the white-and-pink of the three-thorned bush, the occasional flash of carpet flower, exotic white-flowered Mexican poppy, the white *Limeum* and the red *Indigofera*. In their sudden and prolific germination these plants, and the great swathes of sour-smelling Kalahari grass, galvanized into extravagant proliferation by the rain, will smother the young seedlings of the perennials. But no matter: they will soon fade and die, making way for the more durable species.

For a poignantly short while the desert has become a paradise. Soon the sun and the dry air will take their toll, sucking the water from the earth and dehydrating its living things. Within a month the tall grasses are withered, the perennials overcropped and turning brown; the animals and birds, finding little remaining for their comfort, are beginning to drift away, and the sands again lie hot and hostile. But the magic moment will linger in the mind – a bright memory that sustains hope, for there is always a next time.

AGAINST THE ODDS

MANY AND MARVELLOUS ARE THE WAYS IN

WHICH THE LIVING THINGS OF THE DESERT HAVE ADAPTED

TO SURVIVE THE HARSHNESS OF THE THIRSTLANDS.

OF ALL THE CHALLENGES, EXTREME HEAT AND

A FORMIDABLE ABSENCE OF MOISTURE

ARE THE MOST TESTING.

Burchell's sandgrouse is nothing very much to look at, a medium-sized bird, dove-like in flight, much like a long-legged francolin when on the ground. But it has a number of rather special attributes. The adults of the species get the water they need from the plant seeds they eat, but Kalahari seeds tend to be very dry, their moisture content too low to sustain the chicks. So at nesting time the male parent will range 60 kilometres (37 miles) and more across the desert to find water, and when he does he soaks his belly and carries the moisture back to his offspring, who drink from the wet feathers. It's a surprisingly efficient method: the tiny haired barbs (barbules) in the bird's abdominal feathers unfold and interlock to create a kind of sponge that holds up to 40 millilitres (1.4 fluid ounces), more than enough to satisfy the young.

Returning from his 120-kilometre (75-mile) round trip, moreover, he unerringly locates home base, which in itself is quite a feat since the nest is just a scrape in the ground and the pink-coloured female, if she is sitting at the time, is virtually indistinguishable against the red Kalahari sand.

Top *A spotted hyaena at one of the southern park's man-made waterholes.*
Left *A pygmy falcon with its prey, a barking gecko.*
Right *This meerkat sentinel uses a dead tree-trunk as a look-out post.*

The related Namaqua sandgrouse behaves in similar fashion and lives in the same general area, but it doesn't share the same habitat – it more or less confines itself to calcrete outcrops where, again, its speckled plumage provides perfect camouflage.

The sandgrouse is not, in fact, historically indigenous to the southern Kalahari but, like many other exotic species, has been drawn to the area by the availability of borehole water. It rears its young in midsummer, a time of ferociously high temperatures, especially at ground level, and its nest in the open sand receives the full force of the sun. All of which would represent intolerable conditions for most forms of life, but the bird has several answers to the problems of heat and moisture loss. It conserves energy by restricting its activity – foraging and searching for water – to the cooler hours of morning and evening; it creates thermal insulation by fluffing out the feathers on its back; and, astonishingly, it seems to be able to predict which days are going to be especially hot and adjusts

Above *A male Burchell's sandgrouse wets its abdominal feathers, and will carry the moisture back to its chicks. The nest could be up to 60 kilometres (37 miles) away.*
Below *A small flock of sandgrouse settles beside a waterhole.*
Opposite *Blackthorn seedpods develop well before the spring leaf flush.*

its drinking pattern accordingly. Just how it can anticipate temperature levels is something that continues to baffle the experts.

The sandgrouse is just one of many Kalahari species that has developed morphological (that is, in its bodily structure), physiological (bodily functions) and behavioural responses, evolved through natural selection over the millennia, to cope with the extreme demands of desert life.

GROWTH IN ADVERSITY

Unlike animals, the plants of the sandveld cannot move to a better location to escape the harshness of a particular environment. They have to stay where they are and make the best of the conditions. But they are amazingly resilient. Adaptations to their enzymes for instance – those special proteins produced by the body's cells that trigger chemical reactions – enable many of them, incredibly, to withstand temperature fluctuations that range from 16 °C (61 °F) below zero up to a wicked 70 °C (158 °F).

The mechanisms for reducing transpiration – water loss – are complex. One way is for the plant to open its breathing apparatus – the stomata or 'windows' of its leaves – in the cooler hours of the night, when there is more vapour in the desert air. But this is only a partial solution since the plant still has to photosynthesize (convert carbon dioxide into organic compounds), and for this of course it needs sunlight. So some ingenious modifications have evolved. Some species take in carbon dioxide at night and convert it into an acid, which dissolves during the daylight hours to enable photosynthesis to proceed while the stomata remain closed. Other plants have different answers, the most effective of them involving a 'boundary layer' of humid air that surrounds the leaf surface and slows down the rate of water loss.

The rate is further reduced if the stomata are recessed, so marginally but crucially increasing the distance between the open 'windows' and the atmosphere.

However, this delicate arrangement is vulnerable to the desert breezes, which destroy the protective layer and accelerate the loss of moisture (plants, as gardeners know only too well, wilt that much faster in hot and windy conditions). Here again, though, evolutionary selection has come to the rescue, producing structures either on the leaf surface or on the plant as a whole or both: epidermal hairs, thorns, spines, branches which help prevent wind penetration and preserve the boundary layer. Some species – the blackthorn, shepherd's tree and puzzle bush, for example – also cluster together in dense thickets in a collective bid to keep the layer intact.

Others use colour and texture to the same end. The grey camelthorn's shiny leaves, the light-hued ones of the ganna bushes which grow around the edges of the salt pans, and even the hairs of the camelthorn's giant pods, reflect solar radiation, reducing the amount of energy absorbed and therefore the rate of evaporation.

For most of the Kalahari's trees, bushes and shrubs, however, survival depends on the root system, on its ability to penetrate to the deeper levels. There, the moisture remains for longer periods of the year, which not only keeps the plant alive but, importantly, also improves its chances of successful reproduction.

The depth and type of root indicate the plant's survival strategy. The upper Kalahari soil layers, those less than 40 centimetres (16 inches) from the surface, are

exposed to long dry periods and very high temperatures, and the species they sustain tend to be the winter annuals – plants such as *Gisekia pharnacioides* and *Limeum sulcatum* which respond, often dramatically, to the late summer rains and the occasional winter shower. They live happily enough in their niche because there is little competition from the longer-rooted perennials, but the water situation is always precarious and they tend to be short-lived. The slightly deeper zone, that extending 100 centimetres (39 inches) or so beneath the surface, also dries out in winter (though not on the dune crests and slopes), but holds the summer rain for a fair time, sustaining the summer annuals and also *Oxalis* and other winter species.

Deeper still and you'll find the perennials – Lehmann's lovegrass *Eragrostis lehmannia* and the tall Bushman grass *Stipagrostis ciliata*, whose roots reach down about 2 metres (2.2 yards); brandy bush, blackthorn and camelthorn penetrate to even lower levels, some escaping drought conditions by thrusting down

10 metres (11 yards) and more. Access to water is their urgent and overwhelming priority, which you pretty soon discover if you try transplanting, say, a small camelthorn: a seedling just a few centimetres tall has a taproot 2 metres (2.2 yards) and more in length.

For many plants, an extensive lateral system is as important as the taproot. The latter seeks a permanent water supply; the former is more opportunistic, sucking up the rain that all too briefly soaks the ground. The lateral roots also deny water to other, less robust species, effectively killing off competition for a precious and very limited commodity. Camelthorns, bastard umbrella-thorns and cure-worms have lateral roots that snake their way out a full 20 metres (22 yards) and more – an invasion of the soil that creates a spacious naked area around the mother plant. The blackthorn is especially good at out-competing the opposition: only in the wettest years are the annual grasses able to encroach on its preserve. These bare patches, which also serve as natural firebreaks

Above *Broom bushes, set on root pedestals, thrive on the windswept dunes.*
Opposite *A pygmy falcon, its feathers fluffed, fights against the winter cold.*

(a real bonus when summer lightning is around), are strikingly evident when observed from the air.

About a fifth of the southern Kalahari's plants are made up of bulbs, corms and tubers, a group whose members are known as geophytes and which favour the relatively stable fine sands of the pan-surrounds and dune *straats* (streets). They are largely confined to upper soil levels but are well protected from desiccation by their layers of outer tissue. Moreover, they do not spend energy in thrusting long shoots up to the surface. By keeping their food resources on tap, as it were, geophytes are able to sprout in the early summer months, just prior to the first rains and well before the annual plants germinate – and in so doing they take full advantage of a competition-free period. There is, though, a

down-side to an otherwise profitable timetable: they are the only green plants – the only food – available during these weeks and therefore a prime target for the hungry wildlife. Intriguingly, many of them have developed ingenious chemical defence mechanisms to discourage would-be foragers (see page 59).

HOW WARM-BLOODED CREATURES COPE

For the animals of the Kalahari the pre-rain summer months are the most stressful of all. The succulent winter plants that sustained many of the herbivores, large and small, wither and die, leaving little in their place; moisture is an increasingly scarce commodity, and those mechanisms that enable the various types of wildlife to cope with the heat are tested to the full. Just how they do so is, at the most basic level, determined first by whether the species' body temperatures are regulated by outside heat sources (these are the cold-blooded ectotherms, creatures such as insects, snakes and lizards) or internally, by the body itself (the warm-blooded or endothermic mammals and birds). The latter are the most adaptable of living forms, able to survive in most habitats and within a wide air-temperature range. The ectotherms, by contrast, are restricted to an environment and times of day that provide enough external warmth.

Endotherms have stable or almost stable body temperatures, mammals averaging 34–38 °C (93–100 °F), birds 39–42 °C (102–108 °F), both generating body heat by burning up sugars, fats and proteins. But when the outside air gets cold the body begins to lose this heat and the animal must either escape to a warmer micro-climate – a burrow or nest, for instance – or increase its insulation by raising the fur or fluffing the feathers, or produce extra heat through muscle activity. This last is achieved by shivering as well as active movement. In the final resort – that is, if all these fail to keep out the cold – an extra process can sometimes be triggered to burn a special high-energy fat, but this mechanism is restricted to the young and to those animals that go into hibernation (a cold-climate phenomenon).

In the Kalahari, though, the real challenges are those residing at the other end of the temperature spectrum. Heat is the

enemy. And the animals respond in various ways: they escape to a less torrid place, or dump excess body heat by exposing certain areas of the body – the belly or the underwing parts – to the breeze and to the cooler sands, or resort to physiological remedies such as sweating.

A key factor in temperature control is body size. Because of their larger surface area to volume ratios, small animals lose and gain body heat at a faster rate than the

bigger species. There is in fact a direct and universal relationship between size and metabolic rate that is informally known as the 'mouse-to-elephant curve'. A tiny, warm-blooded creature like the hairy-footed gerbil has a rate about 50 times higher, per gram of bodyweight, than a 5 500-kilogram (12 100-pound) elephant. So although the gerbil spends much less *total* energy, the *proportionate* amount of energy it needs to meet its fuel demands

and maintain a stable body temperature is a lot greater. All of which has major consequences in the perennial quest for food and water, and in how the animals contend with the desert's extremes of heat and cold.

Regional adaptations are also significant: it's an interesting fact that Kalahari creatures of all sizes have a 40 per cent or so lower metabolic rate than their fellow-species in the wetter parts of the subcontinent, and thus use up less food and water.

HIDING FROM HEAT AND COLD

Small animals such as rats, shrews and bats make up about two-fifths of the Kalahari's mammal population – something of a testimony to their toughness, resilience and ability to colonize arid areas (or any other region for that matter). Their success is related principally to body size – a rodent heats up very quickly in the desert sun – and to their skill in exploiting a variety of

Left *Meerkats emerge from their burrow, which provides them with warmth as well as security.*
Above *A family of striped mice makes its home among the debris of a collapsed sociable weaver's nest.*

micro-habitats. The southern Kalahari's 17 recorded rodents avoid the heat of the day by remaining in their burrows, where they are comfortable, safe from predators and well insulated against the high temperatures outside. Here they can lose their body heat, the diurnal ones able to cool down before returning to the open. Those burrows that penetrate 30 centimetres (12 inches) and more beneath the surface maintain an ideal temperature, 30–40 °C (86–104 °F), in both summer and winter. The well-sealed chambers are more humid than the air above ground, which brings extra benefits to burrowing animals – they don't lose body moisture through evaporation by having to inhale the dry air outside.

Those desert rodents which are either wholly or partially nocturnal have an easier time of it in summer, but they must of course contend with the bitterly cold winter nights. To do so they have evolved coats of dense fur. Especially snug are the 22-gram (0.8-ounce) big-eared desert mouse *Malacothrix typica* and the bulkier

(65-gram or 2.3-ounce) black-tailed tree-rat *Thallomys nigricauda*, both of which are fully exposed to the winter elements: the former inhabits the open pans, the latter the handsome camelthorn trees. Oddly enough, the tree-rat's thick coat is just as effective in keeping the animal cool in the summer months, reducing the transfer of heat from the air to its body in much the same way as the wool of a sheep. Wool and fur are relatively poor conductors because pockets of air become trapped among the layers, effectively keeping the hot surface away from the cool, moist skin.

Indeed tree-rats have a quite phenomenal capacity for withstanding high temperatures. This is a nocturnal species, though it does emerge into the open in the late afternoon and early morning, foraging close to its home base (it lives on a diet of tree-gum, seeds, berries, roots and insects). The animals are rather difficult to spot, but you can usually tell whether there's a family around by the presence of a 'nest' in the branches, a haphazard affair of twigs that serves as home. The real nest – the breeding area – is less visible, invariably hidden in a hollow or hole in the tree. The rats – very proficient climbers – have long black tails, longer than their ground-living cousins and an adaptation to their arboreal habitat: they help in maintaining balance, and are prehensile, able to grasp

Huddling together is a common enough way of keeping warm in the wintertime desert. Tree-rats do it in their family nests. For the slightly larger ground squirrel and the meerkat (or suricate), endearing little creatures often spotted going about their busy ways in the river-beds, bodily contact is a vital part of the survival strategy. Observations have shown that when half a dozen squirrels crowd up against each

branches. The rats used to be common in the Nossob and Mata Mata areas, but the savage droughts of the recent past have played havoc with the population.

Tree-rats can tolerate air temperatures of around 43 °C (109 °F) for a number of hours at a stretch without apparent discomfort – a remarkable ability. They do so by losing moisture through evaporation, which they can afford because they eat the nutritious and water-rich gum from the bark of the camelthorn. Their nests also offer protection against the heat, though less so than the subterranean burrows of terrestrial rats. Moreover, the moisture evaporation is kept within reasonable limits by the animal's habit of urinating on the nests, which effectively reduces the surrounding vapour pressure. Other species –

Above *This tree-rat has built its nest in the fork of an ancient camelthorn.*
Right *Lions are increasingly nocturnal as desert temperatures rise; this one became active when the sun was well down and the earth had started to cool.*

notably the striped mouse, the only small rodent that is truly diurnal – also survive the intense heat of the day by consuming plant pods, flowers, insects and other food items with a relatively high water content. In contrast, the big-eared desert mouse and the hairy-footed gerbil live almost exclusively on sun-dried seeds and resort to escape-type behaviour. The gerbil spends the hot hours of the day in an elaborate communal burrow system.

other on a freezing night there's a full 40 per cent saving in energy. Many other species use their brothers and sisters as blankets, but the behaviour is especially important to these two diurnal rodents because their coats are rather thin and coarse-textured, adaptations that have evolved to cope with the intense heat of daytime living rather than to provide good insulation against the cold.

Above ground, these animals move in and out of the sun to maintain a reasonably constant body temperature. They also take sand-baths, lying belly-down and splay-legged in a shady patch in an effort to download excess body heat – a type of 'thermal window' exploited by several other species *(see page 65)*. And the ground squirrel has yet another answer to the fierce sun, a built-in one: it carries its

own shade around with it, its large bushy tail serving as a parasol which it waves in gentle arcs, above its back and head, while out feeding. This lowers its temperature by a couple of degrees, so allowing it to forage for longer periods – a distinct advantage over its competitors. The parasol also enables it to stay out during those hours when the large birds of prey, its main enemies, have retired into the cool canopies of

trees. When the open ground becomes just too hot for the squirrel it will retreat into the nearest patch of deep shade, lie on its belly with its legs stretched out fore and aft and throw sand over itself. Meerkats and yellow mongooses do the same thing (hyaenas sometimes go a step further by urinating on the sand to cool it even more). At the other end of the size scale for burrowing animals, and weighing in at 18 and 65 kilograms (40 and 143 pounds) respectively, are the porcupine and aardvark. Though both have low metabolic rates, their insulation is poor. The porcupine's quills provide little warmth. The aardvark, a largely nocturnal insectivore with an almost hairless skin, a humped back, elongated snout and long tongue, gains a measure of protection against the cold from its sheer bulk, but the animal is really designed to lose heat, of which a lot is generated during its frantic demolition of termite mounds. It also uses its short, powerful front limbs to dig for ants' nests deep beneath the surface. The burrow system in which it lives, often built on more than one level, is surprisingly extensive and may have several entrances and chambers. Both species lose a lot of moisture on hot days, making up the deficits by eating foods rich in water: the porcupine's diet comprises roots and bulbs; the aardvark's ants and termites but also wild fruit.

In the perennial effort to conserve energy a number of the smaller Kalahari endotherms, birds as well as mammals, actually lower their body temperatures – some of them, for example, the pouched mouse, by as much as 15 °C (59 °F) – to enter into a state of torpor. The slowing down of the body's metabolism, a phenomenon especially common among rodents, reduces both the need for food (very important in times of scarcity) and the rate at which moisture is lost.

THE ANTELOPE'S ANSWERS

Some of the most striking adaptations to desert conditions have evolved in the large mammals, those which cannot (usually)

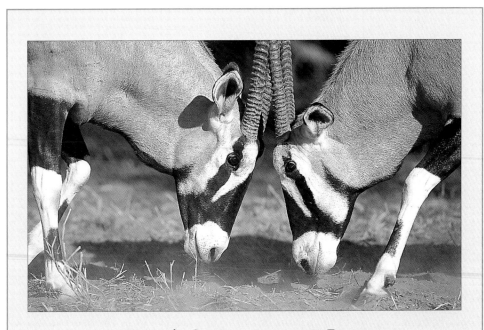

THE BRAIN'S SUPER-EFFICIENT RADIATOR

In the heat of a Kalahari summer's day the gemsbok's body temperature can rise to an incredible 45 °C (113 °F), and does so without ill effect because a vulnerable part of the brain – the all-important temperature control centre called the hypothalamus – is protected by a feature known as the carotid rete. This curious structural mechanism is present in a number of animals in non-desert as well as desert regions, among them certain types of gazelle, sheep, a variety of ungulates and even some cats. The feature consists of a maze of fine blood vessels that, together, act as an efficient heat-exchange unit. Warm arterial blood flowing from the heart to the brain passes through the network, which is surrounded by veins that carry blood cooled through evaporation in the nasal area. The interaction of warm arterial and cool venous blood in the rete lowers the former's temperature by a few life-giving degrees (this is termed a contra-current heat exchange) before entering the brain. Contrary to earlier scientific perceptions, this mechanism only comes into play when the animal is relaxed. During flight, fight and other times of stress it pants in order to cool its body, but panting wastes a lot of moisture and, in the superheated desert, is used only in emergencies.

escape into burrows and are exposed to the elements day and night, summer and winter. Here in the Kalahari, where there is so little moisture and drinking water is at a premium, every activity has to be geared to conserving resources.

The antelope's first defence against the hot summer sun is to retreat to whatever shade is available (the fleet-footed steenbok sometimes goes further by retiring into an aardvark or porcupine burrow). Prime refuges are the larger acacia trees, within which there are convective currents, the hot air rising on the outside of the canopy and descending through the central parts to the ground below. The various species, though, have slightly different needs and behavioural patterns

depending on the area. In the South African park, for example, gemsbok make more use of shade than wildebeest, probably because the former get their moisture from plants while the latter drink water, which is readily available from the park's many artificial waterholes.

A more subtle adaptation to desert conditions are the light-hued, shiny coats of antelope such as springbok, gemsbok and steenbok, colour and texture combining to reflect direct solar radiation. This protective feature is reinforced by the whiteness of the animals' bellies, a barrier to redirect radiation from the ground.

Then again, all these open-plains species choose their physical orientation with careful precision, so positioning themselves

that the smallest possible area of their bodies is exposed to the sunshine. The springbok's white rump-patch offers an added bonus, helping reflect up to 95 per cent of the sun's rays from its body – an efficient energy-saver indeed. Exactly what the gemsbok's dark rump-patch was designed for, though, is still anyone's guess. It may be vestigial in value, the adaptive need for it long since gone; or, because it is such a contrasting colour to the animal's facial markings, it may serve as a follow-me sign to other herd members.

The Kalahari's antelope tend to have thin coats and hides, outer coverings developed for easy heat loss rather than for insulation. The adaptation is especially valuable to the springbok, whose only

defence against predators is to run as fast and far as it can, its body temperature soaring to a dangerous 41 °C (106 °F) while the chase is on. If the heat were not quickly dissipated the animal would simply keel over and die. It survives because it pants profusely, its heart pumps blood to areas just under the skin and the heat is downloaded into the cooler air. The springbok's poor insulation, incidentally, probably accounts for its generally larger size in the Kalahari: elsewhere, in the milder Karoo, for instance, it spends more of its energy keeping warm, less on the growth process.

These animals also sweat in order to regulate their temperatures, a faculty well developed in mammals but especially so in the larger species (the smaller ones,

rodents for instance, cannot spare the water consumed in this efficient but highly wasteful response). The sweating mechanism, though, is automatically switched off when the animal becomes dehydrated – a limiting factor fortunately (for the prey) shared by most large carnivores. In short, it's simply too dangerous to indulge in violent activity when air temperatures are hovering around the 40 °C (104 °F) mark, and for this reason you'll seldom if ever see a cheetah hunting in the heat of a Kalahari day. And of course the park's rangers, equipped as they are with vehicles and helicopters under no such constraint, are very careful to take ambient temperature and humidity into account when on game-capturing expeditions.

Above *Springbok in the Auob valley after good rains. The white rump-patch is an energy saver: it helps reflect sunlight from the animal's body.*
Overleaf *Wildebeest herd on trek.*

When desert antelope, some of them, are under water-stress and cannot afford the moisture that sweating demands, they simply allow their body temperatures to rise so that less heat needs to be dissipated – yet another remarkable adaptation. The mechanism is at its most impressive in the eland and especially the gemsbok, both of which are big animals that can stand longer periods of high body heat than the smaller bovids. One series of experiments

revealed that the animals' early-morning
temperatures can be as low as 34 °C
(93 °F) but that as the day wears on their
body heat increases to around 41 °C
(106 °F) (a little less in the gemsbok)
which, for the 1 000-kilogram (2 200-
pound) eland, means a retention of about
6 000 kilojoules (1 430 calories) of heat
and thus conserves 10 litres (350 fluid
ounces) or so of water that would otherwise have been sweated out.

Even more extraordinary is the gemsbok's temperature, which, when dehydra-
tion threatens, actually rises above the
ambient level – to 45 °C (113 °F) (high
enough to kill other mammals), so that
heat is lost through conduction and radiation (*see box, page 66*).

THE DESERT BIRDS

Many of the southern Kalahari's birds are
nomadic seed-eaters. Weavers, finchlarks,
doves, sandgrouse, canaries come and go

depending on how good the rains have been and the quality of the vegetation. Indeed, of the South African park's 264 recorded species, fully 152 are irregular inhabitants, vagrants that are common in some years, entirely absent in others. Thirty-four more are regular visitors, and a relatively modest 78 are present throughout the year.

A number of migrants stop over in the southern Kalahari, notably during the sporadic boom periods. The heat and the summer moisture brought by rain showers trigger population explosions among the insects and rodents. Stinkbugs and crickets, dung beetles, grasshoppers, caterpillars, Kalahari moths, swarms of African migrant and monarch butterflies and all manner of other creeping, crawling and flying creatures, together with the sudden proliferation of rats and mice, are a magnet for battalions of Abdim's and white storks, harlequin quails, predatory yellowbilled kites from Europe and the Middle East, steppe buzzards from Central Asia, the occasional Wahlberg's eagle and many others.

The seed-eaters are always on the move, seeking out the scattered, isolated patches that have been favoured by the rain and staying only so long as the food lasts – anything from a day or so to an entire summer. The seeds provide nourishment but not much moisture and so the birds flock, sometimes in their hundreds, around what standing water is available, which in this wilderness is usually confined to the borehole-supplied drinking places. Here they take their fill, but at considerable risk: airborne predators such as falcons home in on the tempting targets; jackals, wild cats and other terrestrial hunters manoeuvre for an easy kill. These artificial sources, by the by, have significantly affected distribution patterns among some species: today, sandgrouse and doves, for example, are seen in greater numbers and for longer periods than in the past, before the boreholes made their appearance.

Opposite, above *The cheetah's markings provide effective camouflage.*
Opposite, below *A male yellow canary; seed-eaters are common in the Kalahari in years of good rainfall.*
Right *For the ostrich, drinking is a laborious process.*

THE KALAHARI'S APARTMENT BLOCK

Among the more common, and remarkable, sights in the Kalahari are the huge communal nests of the sociable weaver (**opposite, top right**). When you drive towards the South African park from Upington you'll see telephone poles, windmill towers and camelthorns festooned with these structures, built entirely from straws the weavers gather from the dust-dry veld. These they knit into an interlocking system of rooms that can weigh up to 1 000 kilograms (2,200 pounds), contain 50 and more individual chambers and provide a comfortable home for 300 paired birds. The structures are safe, protected against heat, cold and rain and, if well looked after, can survive intact for decades at a stretch. Interestingly, though, it seems that the weavers only carry out repairs when there's a fair amount of grass available. In the drought-stricken years between 1984 and 1988, for instance, there was minimal maintenance and the nests along the Auob and Nossob rivers and elsewhere deteriorated badly. Those that did receive attention were poorly renovated, with inferior dubbeltjie twigs instead of the preferred grass stalks.

The tree-nests are usually sited in the lower branches, where they get the maximum amount of shade. The chambers occupy the bottom part of the nest to make them as inaccessible as possible to both airborne and climbing predators and to provide the easiest way in for the residents themselves. Moreover, by using the camelthorn and sometimes the shepherd's tree as their base, the birds are lessening a major risk: these tree species have extensive lateral root systems that discourage plant growth, so creating the natural firebreaks necessary for the tree's, and the nest's, survival (see also page 58).

The weaver's nests are superbly insulated. Observations show that, while outside temperatures fluctuate by as much as 25 °C (77 °F) between day and night, those inside the structure vary by no more than 6 °C (43 °F), and that they never fall below 15 °C (59 °F) in winter or rise above 31 °C (88 °F) in summer. To create even more warmth during the chilly periods the birds will huddle together, up to five crowding into a single chamber. On summer nights and during their daytime siestas, on the other hand, an individual will, if it possibly can, find and keep a space all to itself. The nest therefore minimizes summertime evaporation and enables the weavers to save a lot of energy and water. A permanent home also gives them a headstart in the breeding stakes: they are a

highly opportunistic species, able to lay their eggs just six days after a rainstorm (the shortest response period recorded for any desert-adapted bird) and in favourable times will produce up to four broods in a season. The chicks remain in the parental nesting chamber (**above, left**) for about three weeks after hatching by which time they are able to fly.

So well adapted and successful are sociable weavers that it is little wonder they attract hangers-on. The tiny pygmy falcon (**below**), which could not survive the rigours of winter without the thermal comforts of a good nest, uses the weaver's chambers for warmth (its presence is easily detected by the white faecal cakes it leaves at the entrance). Although

the falcons normally feed on lizards and insects, they do occasionally seize a weaver chick, but this is very much the exception rather than the rule: it simply would not be in the raptor's interest to destroy the domestic system on which its very life depends.

Another predator that invades the nest, but with more harmful intent, is the Cape cobra Naja nivea. By moving methodically from chamber to chamber it can and sometimes does wipe out an entire colony, but being a cold-blooded species its hunting forays are restricted to the warm summer months. Honey badgers are also unwelcome intruders, and can destroy the whole structure in their efforts to get at the eggs and chicks.

Some seed-eaters also feed on insects, which provide moisture as well as food. A few need neither open water nor insects in order to survive, among them the scalyfeathered finch and the elegant, wader-like doublebanded courser. The latter is especially notable for the way it copes with the harsh conditions: not only does it thrive in the waterless terrain but it seems to prefer places that lack ground cover, actually moving away from the well-vegetated patches to areas where it can clearly detect those insects it prefers. The courser lays just one egg at a time, producing perhaps four offspring in a year (it is one of the few birds not governed by a breeding calendar), the adults taking hour-long turns to incubate the egg. This kind of shared parenting is essential to the species' wellbeing since the nest receives the full force of the sun, and the bird needs regular cooling-down spells in the shade. When the heat becomes too intense, as it invariably does on summer days, even an hour is too much and, at these times, it allows its body temperature to rise.

In fact the Kalahari's birds respond in much the same way as the mammals to the challenges of heat and cold. They are, though, blessed with insulating feathers and slightly higher body temperatures that enable them to cope with a hotter environment and, therefore, to forage for longer periods. This also, most probably, accounts for their ability to survive in arid places without the benefit of an insulating burrow.

But there are some exceptions. Anteating chats *Myrmecocichla formicivora* roost and nest in disused aardvark homes, and sociable weavers (*see box, page 72*) build huge, many-chambered nests above the ground. For the rest, though, small birds such as the 27-gram (0.95-ounce) scalyfeathered finch handle the freezing winter nights by huddling together, competing vigorously for the cosiest middle berth on a perch. Those species which occur singly or in pairs survive the cold because selection has increased their body size – the Kalahari's korhaans, both the black and the redcrested, are bigger than most other members of their genera elsewhere.

Like mammals, birds use shade to regulate their temperatures. On superheated summer days you'll often see Namaqua doves, sandgrouse and even vultures taking their ease on the ground at the base of a tree rather than, as one might expect, in the branches. By doing so they can download their body heat directly and quickly

Opposite *A pair of redheaded finches;*
the male is on the right.
Above *The wader-like spotted dikkop.*
The species is mainly nocturnal; during
good rains its mournful call is a familiar
sound of the night-time desert.

onto the sand (which is a better conductor
than air). They will also let their wings
droop to expose the naked underwing
'thermal windows'. The sandgrouse, indeed, performs this ritual above her offspring while facing into the wind, creating
a venturi-type airflow around the chicks.
The ostrich, at the opposite end of the size
spectrum, takes a similar approach, erect-
ing its feathers and either lowering or raising its wings, all of which allows the cooler
air to circulate. The mobile umbrella so

created is a godsend to its newly hatched
young. Come the cold night and the birds
depress their feathers firmly against their
bodies to trap the warmer air.

Birds cannot sweat, and little water passes through their skin and feathers. They do
pant in order to get rid of heat, but use the
technique sparingly because rapid breathing wastes energy. Some species, the
ostrich among them, lower their temperatures by employing what is known as gular
flutter: at the back of the mouth, in the
gular area, is a thin-skinned chamber full
of blood vessels, and by twitching the
chamber's muscles while keeping the beak
open the bird pumps air in and out of the
pouch – which has the same effect as panting but without the energy-intensive use of
the lungs. As a last resort, when the air
temperature climbs to near-intolerable

levels, a few species will urinate on their
legs to cool themselves down. Many
rodents, including the ground squirrel, do
more or less the same thing when they sali-
vate and lick their fur, though this is so
costly in terms of moisture that they keep
the practice to a bare minimum.

THE COLD-BLOODED SPECIES

The ectotherms of the Kalahari – insects,
reptiles, amphibians – are for the most part
reliant on sunlight for their energy needs,
which makes every evening a time of reckoning: when the sun goes down their body
temperatures fall, and so does their metabolic rate. So most of them tend to be out
and about in the daytime hours, many
extending their active periods in summer
into the warm hours of early darkness.

Insects comprise four-tenths of the southern Kalahari's wildlife species, a bewildering diversity in which certain families are particularly conspicuous.

Everywhere you'll see the mounds of red earth constructed by the desert's termites, tiny (half-centimetre or 0.2-inch) creatures that have been around since the age of the dinosaurs, living in vast colonies that can number a million and more, foraging ceaselessly for the dead vegetable matter – leaves, grass, wood – on which they live. In doing so they provide a significant, even vital food source for other life forms ranging from lizards through birds to foxes.

The way in which the termites prepare their food is a complicated and fascinating process. Essentially, they gather cellulose material quite unpalatable to any other species, take it underground and 'cultivate' a special, mushroom-type fungus (termitomyces) to break it down, thus releasing the nitrogen, proteins and energy locked into the dead matter. It's a remarkable symbiotic relationship: the termites cannot absorb the lignin the plant-matter contains, but pass it out in their waste, depositing it in a 'garden' where the fungus consumes and digests it. The termites then eat the fungus.

The termitarium is also extraordinary. Its architectural design differs from species to species, some built under the surface, others above in various shapes – humped, steepled, turreted. But all have an infinity of passageways and chambers, all are ingeniously ventilated by convection-generated air currents, and all maintain constant atmospheric conditions: a temperature that stays in the 29–31 °C (84–88 °F) range and a 100 per cent humidity level.

Just as well organized are the colonies themselves, divided strictly according to function into soldiers (which defend the nest and its residents), workers (which build and forage) and sexed individuals which, when the weather is exactly right, usually just before the summer rain,

Left *These mounds, in the Nossob valley, have been constructed by the snouted harvester termite.*
Opposite, above *The 'fur' of this scarab beetle enables it to remain active longer into the night.*
Opposite, below *Its cousin the harvester termite builds an underground burrow.*

emerge as winged nymphs (alates) and fly off in their multitudes in their bid to ensure the future. The great majority fail, falling victim to birds and other predators.

Most of the termites in the southern Kalahari are of the harvester variety *Hodotermes mossambicus*, which build their nests underground, and which are unusual in that they have eyes to see. But the area does have its mounds, mainly in the clay-rich areas, structures erected by the snouted harvester termites *Trinervitermes trinervoides*, their common name a reference to the soldier's elongated head.

These insects, unlike their *Hodotermes* cousins, use a chemical irritant (the soldiers produce sticky threads of noxious, terpene-based secretions) rather than their jaws (which are weak) to deter their enemies – though it has little effect on their chief predator, the aardwolf. The latter is a medium-sized (50-kilogram or 110-pound), highly specialized nocturnal mammal distinguished by its thick mane, which it raises in a pronounced display when alarmed or excited. Specialization does have its advantages, of course, but the aardwolf goes to extremes and sometimes suffers the consequences: it virtually restricts its food intake to the *Trinervitermes* termites, which are one of the few of their kind found foraging in great numbers at night and in the open. The animal, with its long wide tongue, broad palate and a stomach adapted to digest large quanti-

ties of their chemical secretion, can consume up to 300 000 of the insects in a single night. Nevertheless, unlike the aardvark and pangolin, both of which are expert diggers capable of demolishing the hard mounds, aardwolves must forage on the surface, and on cold winter nights the termites, sensibly, stay underground. It is during this period that many of the insectivores lose their cubs to, and some adults die from, starvation. Fortunately, it is also at this time that the *Hodotermes* termites emerge to offer an alternative food source – albeit one that is about two-thirds less substantial. The hard outer covering of *Hodotermes* workers is pigmented enough to withstand direct sunlight, and they for-

age in the early mornings and late afternoons – about the only times that one has a chance of spotting the shy aardwolf.

Then there are the beetles, an uncountable number and variety of them – they comprise the largest of the faunal orders, totalling more than 300 000 different species throughout the world. Especially intriguing are the dung beetles, those most efficient of scavengers *(see page 122)*, and some of the tenebrionids, a group characterized mainly by their dark colours. The latter includes the well-known *toktokkie*, a large wingless species which identifies itself and attracts potential mates by knocking rapidly and sharply on the ground with its abdomen, a universal and

familiar sound of the veld. Notable, too, but in a quite different way, are the region's millipedes, multi-jointed arthropods that emerge from burrows only after the rare downpours. Some of them are monsters, measuring 20 centimetres (8 inches) and more from end to end.

Another creature which lives much of its life out of sight beneath the ground, and whose noisy presence is even more a part of the African scene than the *toktokkie*, is the cicada. Its strident, high-pitched call is produced by vibrating a pair of drum-like abdominal organs, filling the summer air in a ceaseless symphony.

For sheer visual appeal few insects can match the tiny red velvet mite *Dino-thrombium tinctorium*, bright scarlet in colour and encased in a dense, soft cover-ing of hairs that has the appearance and texture of velvet. The mites, which live underground and whose larvae parasitize life forms ranging from scorpions up to the large mammals before dropping off to become free-living adults, are seen at their most prolific in the early morning after a shower. They are quite harmless, and usu-ally disappear before the day heats up.

The southern Kalahari has its fair share of arachnids, though many of the species have not been properly studied and indeed many more have yet to be discovered. Among the most poisonous are the button spiders – in particular the one known as the black widow. This creature can deliver a venomous bite that affects the nervous system but is rarely fatal, even when untreated. More dangerous, certainly more painful, are the stings of some of the desert's scorpions. Here there are two main families: the Scorpionidae, which have lethal-looking pincers, slender stings and by and large crush their prey (usually soft-bodied insects) to death; and the Buthidae, which are the ones to avoid. Their pincers are innocuous enough but the toxin from the thick, powerful stings can be deadly. The most poisonous of the scorpions is *Parabuthus granulosa*, which

Opposite *Tiny red velvet mites.*
Right, above *The fiscal shrike, an aggressive little bird that hunts insects.*
Right, below *The everpresent cicada, whose ceaseless, high-pitched call fills the summer air.*

type and its summer days become unbearably hot, most insects resort to normal practice and simply escape underground.

But in cold weather some species – the flying beetles and the bees among them – enjoy a degree of thermal independence, operating in air temperatures that would be much too chilly for other species by twitching their flight muscles to generate body heat. Others have evolved protective insulation: the nocturnal scarab *Sparrmannia flava* has a dense coat of 'fur' which enables it to remain active when the thermometer falls below 25 °C (77 °F).

Professor Anna Rosa, from the University of Bonn, has discovered another, and especially notable, insect adaptation to the cold. Working on the dunes in the Twee Rivieren area she recorded that, during the dry season one particular nocturnal tenebrionid *Parastizopus armaticeps* often hunkered down in a burrow with up to eight of its fellow beetles, an aggregation that probably raises vapour pressure, reduces each individual's water loss and so enhances the chances of survival. She also noted that two other tenebrionid species, *Gonopus agrestis* and the smaller *Herpiscius* species, got together in the same fashion, and that Herpiscius's contact with its larger companion was life-sustaining. This is the first-ever documented example of interspecific insect huddling.

SNAKES AND LIZARDS

The southern Kalahari's reptiles, in contrast to its mammals and birds, rarely suffer from heat stress during the dry summer months. Notable among the region's snakes is the handsome Cape cobra, whose deep yellow body is easily discernible against the red of the dunes. The species is highly poisonous and widely feared, but like most of the family it is docile enough, preferring escape to confrontation, and only becomes aggressive when defending itself. Some cobras are able to 'spit' their venom, usually aiming at the eyes, the liquid dissipating into a fine spray that can carry about 2 metres (2.2 yards).

Rather more common, and more dangerous, is the puff adder, which is slow-moving, difficult to spot in its sandy environment, and able to strike with lightning speed, its long curved fangs biting deep and then quickly withdrawn. Curiously,

emerges on hot, windy nights to prey on insects and rodents (it also shows little compunction in eating its own kind).

Like the mammals and birds, the upper limits of an ectotherm's metabolic rate are determined by body temperature, that of most insects falling within the 29–38 °C (84–100 °F) range. So their adult life cycles are geared largely to the summer, riding out the winters as eggs, pupae and larvae. But they still have to maintain a stable reservoir of body heat, and to do so they pop in and out of the shade in much the same way as the endotherms, though this of course places limitations on their foraging areas.

But not in every case: some species manage to overcome these restrictions. The ant *Camponotus* takes advantage of the vertical variations in air temperature, climbing up grass stalks to get into the cooler levels, an accomplishment that enables it to forage even when the sand below is a blistering 70 °C (158 °F) and there's no shade nearby. Again, observations in the Namib Desert show that the long legs of some tenebrionid beetles can raise their bodies high enough to reach the slightly more tolerable air.

These heat-beating tricks are the exception, and they are not always successful: in the final analysis, when the Kalahari runs to the adder uses its venom only on warm-blooded species: lizards and other ecto-therms are swallowed whole. Other local snakes include the small horned adder, the mole snake *Pseudaspis cana* and a variety of sand snakes (*Psammophis* species).

Two species of tortoise, the Kalahari tent tortoise *Psammobates oculifer* and the much larger leopard or mountain tortoise *Geochelone pardalis*, occur in the region but are seen only during the rainy season. Rather surprisingly the sandveld also sus-tains a modest array of amphibians – six frog species in all – whose moist skins, one might think, would seem to exclude them from arid areas. But there they are, noisily present in their thousands after the first good downpour of summer.

Among the southern Kalahari's several types of lizard are two fossorial, or burrow-ing, species: *Typhlosaurus gariepensis* and *T. lineatus*, respectively the Gariep and striped blind legless skinks. They are extra-ordinary creatures: neither can see and both have lost their legs in their evolutionary

Opposite, above *Skinks in courtship.*
Opposite, below *The sluggish puff adder, a common desert snake.*
Right *The rare gymnogene.*
Below *The deadly Cape cobra.*

adaptation to living and moving just beneath the surface of the desert. Both are streamlined for their subterranean life-style. They also have a divided frontal bone in the skull, which looks rather spade-like and does indeed help them shovel their way through the sand around the vege-tated dune ridges. The Gariep is yellow, the striped species varies in hue (an all-black specimen occasionally occurs). Other, more conventional lizards can, like the chameleon but not so dramatically, actually change colour, becoming darker during the cooler periods in order better to absorb the sun's radiation and gain body heat. Conversely they can also modify their shape to lose heat, adjusting their bodies to present a slimmer and deeper profile to the blistering sun. And, in much the same way as some of the tenebrionid beetles, they raise themselves up on their legs to take advantage of the cooler air: even a centimetre (0.4 inches) can make a signifi-cant difference – as much as 15 degrees.

HUNTERS OF THE DAY

OF THE KALAHARI'S LARGER ANIMALS,

ONLY THE SLEEK AND GRACEFUL CHEETAH

HUNTS DURING THE DAYLIGHT HOURS. BUT THERE

IS PLENTY OF DRAMA LOWER DOWN ON THE SIZE SCALE,

AMONG THE VIVERRIDS, THE RODENTS,

REPTILES, BIRDS AND INSECTS.

The most spectacular of the desert park's predators is the cheetah. It is also the smallest and arguably most beautiful of the big cats, and the swiftest of all land mammals, able to cover the ground at close to 100 kilometres (62 miles) an hour in short, explosive bursts.

The animal is superbly designed for speed, graced by a sinuous, streamlined body, small head, deep keel-like chest, long and powerful legs and a substantial tail that helps maintain perfect balance during the zigzag chase. But physical specialization has its drawbacks. The cheetah has little stamina: during the lightning-fast sprint its body temperature soars, a lot of energy is lost, and the effort cannot be sustained for more than a few seconds. If the animal doesn't manage to catch its prey within 400 metres (440 yards),

Top *The Lilacbreasted roller.*
Left *The ground agama risks life and limb when making its territorial display from a prominent perch.*
Right *After leaving the maternal group, young male cheetahs will often hunt in partnership with a sibling.*

perhaps 600 metres (660 yards), it gives up. Its kill rate in the southern Kalahari is about two out of every seven attempts (which compares favourably with the lion's one in six) but even after a successful chase it cannot eat straightaway. It must rest for a good few minutes, exhausted and panting, until it regains its breath – time enough for the vultures and other scavengers to move in. And most Kalahari chases go the full distance. In other reserves the vegetation is dense enough for the cat to get within 50 metres (55 yards) or so of its target without being detected. Here, on the sandveld, there is very little cover.

Nor is the cheetah a robust animal. It does not have the brute strength and aggression of the other big carnivores, the leopards and the lions. It also lacks retractable claws, which puts it at a serious disadvantage in confrontations with better-armed competitors. Other elements, too, have been sacrificed to swift movement over the ground: it cannot rotate the wrists of its fore-limbs, for instance – an adaptation that does help stabilize the animal during its first furious dash, but also prevents it from the acrobatic twisting and turning needed when its antelope prey changes direction at the last moment.

Above and opposite *Cheetahs hunt during the daylight hours, a time when other large carnivores – competitors such as lion, leopard and spotted hyaena – are hiding from the heat. The hunt itself is a dramatic sequence of stalk, lightning-fast sprint, and kill.*

Moreover, the cat's relatively light body (it weighs in at around 40 kilograms or 88 pounds), its weak jaws, small teeth and basically gentle disposition render it curiously submissive to other meat-eaters, and it is often robbed of its kill by spotted

hyaenas, by the other big cats and occasionally even by the brown hyaena, an animal not known for its assertiveness. (By contrast, the smaller carnivores, notably jackals, give the cheetah a wide berth: they know just how fast it is and rarely approach closer than 30 metres.)

The cheetah therefore minimizes the chances of conflict over food by hunting during those times when most competing carnivores are inactive, immobilized by the desert heat. It still has to contend with the voracious vultures, though, and here there is little it can do except drag the carcass into the nearest patch of shade and eat

as quickly as it can. In the Kalahari its favoured prey is the springbok, and for a short period during the lambing season the cats have a fairly easy time of it but soon enough – within a month of birth – the lambs are as mobile as their parents and the hunt becomes a lot more difficult.

However, the southern Kalahari's cheetah do not restrict their diet to these graceful antelope: some specialize in other types of prey. One pair of males near the park's Nossob camp, for example, were expert killers of adult gemsbok – a large animal, and a formidable opponent for the nimble but lightly armed cats. Depending on the

season and the availability of food, they will also hunt wildebeest (again, a tough customer), hartebeest, duiker, steenbok, ostriches, bat-eared foxes and springhares.

Female cheetahs live independent and solitary lives, their only company the latest litter of perhaps five or six cubs. The male is needed only for breeding purposes: the mother is quite capable of looking after her offspring without help, and will lead them over long distances along the river reaches in search of prey. In fact, she is obliged to roam far and wide because the springbok, her major food source, is a highly mobile animal. Her home range will overlap with those of other cheetahs but there seems to be little consciousness of territory: she tolerates intrusion, simply avoiding direct contact with her peers. At some point, usually about 18 months after their birth, the cubs will leave the family circle to wander the sandveld as a mixed-sex group. In due course the males pair up or get together in a threesome to hunt, to scent-mark and defend their turf.

The Nossob and Auob river-beds, which sustain relatively large numbers of spring-bok and are fairly free of other large carni-vores, provide a better home for cheetahs than most other southern African habitats – and, because vegetation is so sparse, they offer the visitor superb viewing opportuni-ties, perhaps the best in Africa.

DRAMA IN MINIATURE

The cheetah is undoubtedly the most eye-catching of the Kalahari's daytime hunters. Indeed, if one discounts the seldom-seen wild dog, it is the region's only consistently diurnal large carnivore: the other preda-tors operate mostly at night. But there's plenty happening lower down on the size scale, among the viverrids, the birds, the rodents and invertebrates. You'll find just as much drama, and not a little ingenuity, on the small stage if you're patient and observe closely.

The spider *Ammoxenus psammodromus* hunts termites over the open ground, but does so in a curiously selective way. He spends much of his life buried in the soft sand, emerging when hungry to scour the surface for his prey. He may meet the odd stray harvester termite, which he will ignore, going into action only when he finds a colony of foragers. He will then run among the insects, over their bodies some-times, without provoking any apparent dis-turbance, his presence unperceived because he does nothing to trigger the chemical reactions necessary for detection – until he selects a particular victim. This he will kill with exquisite precision, deliv-ering his paralyzing bite to a point just behind the head. If he miscalculates, the termite will have time to sound the alarm, releasing a warning pheromone that sends the colony into a frenzy of escape activity. If successful, which he invariably is, the spider buries himself belly-up beneath the sand and eats the termite from below.

The wider Kalahari's spiders come in a great many shapes and sizes and display a huge diversity of habit, habitat and hunt-ing behaviour. The field has not been properly researched and our knowledge is limited (in fact many species almost cer-tainly still await discovery), but we have records of arachnids that 'navigate' by the position of the sun (the wolf spider is one); 'fish' in the slow-moving waters of the Okavango swamps far to the north; live in extensive colonies, and 'fly' through the air on threads of silk, sometimes over immense distances (this method of travel is known as 'ballooning').

Below *The nocturnal giant ground gecko.*
Right *After the kill. The cheetah is a superb hunter, its success rate in the Kalahari is a remarkable two in seven attempts (compared to the lion's one in six). However, compared to other larger predators, the cheetah has sacrificed strength for speed.*

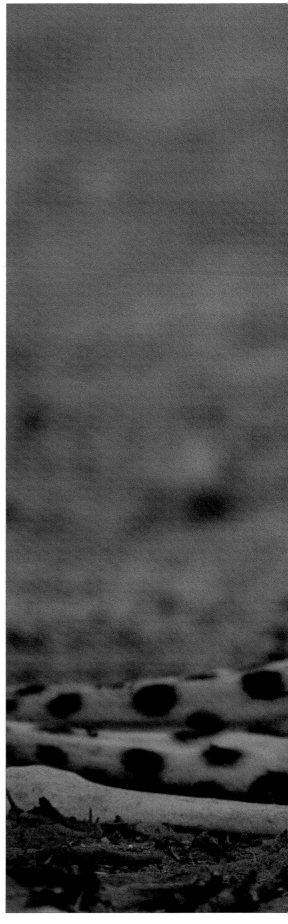

In the dunelands of the southern region the arid, open terrain favours mobile varieties rather than those that live and catch their prey on webs. It is also, predictably, the kind of country where you'll find a preponderance of burrowers, prominent among which are the trapdoor spiders that create especially cosy underground homes for themselves, hideaways protected by silk linings that keep them free of both water and the rigours of the outside environment. Desert spiders can go for extensive periods – some as long as six months – without food. So can the scorpions, which live for the most part on the soft-bodied insects that they detect through the hypersensitive hairs on their bodies and pincers, sensors that pick up the minutest vibrations and air currents.

The Kalahari region contains 27 recorded species of lizard and, like other carnivore groups, their hunting strategies may either be of the free-roaming or the 'sit-and-wait' kind. Notable is the striped sandveld lizard *Nucras tessellata*, which ranges widely in search of scorpions, spiders and

beetles, digging them out of their daytime burrows. By contrast, its spotted cousin *Pedioplanis lineoocellata* hides behind a bush, now and again darting out to grab an unsuspecting insect that is, itself, a widely foraging species. And so it goes on, up the food chain, the one strategy dependent on the other: the mobile *Nucras* is preyed upon by sit-and-wait carnivores such as pygmy falcons and greater kestrels, birds that watch from their high, open perches; the static *Pedioplanis* usually falls victim to honey badgers, jackals, such raptors as the pale chanting goshawk and to other wide-ranging carnivores. An especially efficient predator of foraging lizards, and perhaps the prince of the wider Kalahari's sit-and-waiters, is the horned adder, a snake that hides just beneath the sand, with only its well-camouflaged eyes and curious horns protruding. It lies there patiently, hour after hour, and then strikes with incredible speed and lethal effect at the first unsuspecting passer-by that comes along.

Then there's the aptly named barking gecko *Ptenopus garrulus*. On early sum-

mer evenings this small lizard sits at the entrance to its burrow, using it as a kind of echo chamber for the strange 'chick-chick-chick' noise it makes. The chorus of thousands gives voice in the hour after sunset and, like the high-pitched chirping of the cicadas, it is a familiar and enduring sound of the desert. The gecko also waits for his prey to come along, but sometimes, when rain is imminent and the nymph termites emerge to fill the air, temptation becomes too much for him and, throwing caution to the winds, he dashes out to gobble the swarming insects. The consequences can be fatal: he is not by nature a forager. Unaccustomed to the demands and dangers of life in the open, he remains oblivious of the watching predator – a falcon perhaps, or a shrike – that doesn't include termites in its diet but knows all about the lizard's weakness and is lurking in the wings for just such an opportunity.

One of the less attractive of the Kalahari's hunters – albeit a microscopic one, but a hunter nevertheless and very efficient too – is the blood-sucking sand

Opposite *An African wild cat hunts rodents among the crevices and crannies of one of the Auob's calcrete ridges.*
Above *A praying mantis atop a grey camelthorn tree.*
Right *The rednecked falcon, rather rare in the southern Kalahari and much sought by visiting bird-watchers.*

tampan, a quite extraordinary little creature that is the scourge of domestic animals of the surrounding farmlands, and of shade-seeking visitors to the region. The tick-like tampan, which lives in colonies of myriads, cannot cope with the high temperatures of the open desert terrain (the maximum it is able to tolerate is 55 °C or 131 °F) and retreats into the shaded ground around trees – it normally positions itself 20 centimetres (8 inches) or so below the surface – to wait in ambush for the first luckless mammal to seek relief in the same cool spot. The insects are equipped with sensitive carbon dioxide receptors (sited on the front set of their

appendages), and can also detect move-ment. As soon as an animal approaches they come up to the surface in their multi-tudes and, guided by their receptors, home in on and fasten themselves to their host, voraciously drinking its blood. Their saliva contains a weak neurotoxin that anaes-thetizes the flesh, so the victim is usually quite unaware of their presence – which can often be lethal to those who remain too long in the shade (cattle have been known to die from exsanguination and from the debilitating ulcers that can devel-op from the bites). But as soon as the ani-mal makes a move to leave, the tampans drop off – an unusual reaction within the tick family but absolutely essential to this heat-sensitive species. All of which helps explain why desert animals often choose to shelter under modest-looking trees and bushes in preference to the large, deep-shade specimens.

MEERKAT AND MONGOOSE

The most social and, in human perception, certainly the most delightful of the southern Kalahari's daytime carnivores is the suricate or meerkat (*Suricata suricatta*), a member of the viverrid group that also embraces the mongooses. The small, bright-eyed, pixie-faced, alert, perennially inquisitive little creatures live in bands, which vary in number from half-a-dozen individuals to around 30, in underground burrows with several entrances. These they usually build themselves, but they're not too choosy: they will make use of homes abandoned by ground squirrels; even, sometimes, share a lived-in squirrel warren. Nor do they always return to the same place if they are out and about when twilight comes, choosing instead to build a temporary refuge or take over a conveniently handy shelter for the night. For defence, the meerkat has evolved a remarkable early-warning system, key ingredient of which is the posting of sentries (*see page 49*).

Less sociable and somewhat smaller are the southern Kalahari's three species of mongoose: the slender, the yellow and the seldom seen banded. Indeed the slender mongoose, sometimes called the black-tipped (a reference to the dark end to its tail) is most often seen hunting alone, using stealth to catch the rodents and other small vertebrates that comprise its diet. Like all mongooses, it is a highly efficient killer of snakes, even the biggest and most poisonous ones. The more commonly seen yellow mongoose, distinguished by its attractively bushy white-tipped tail, is also a loner when foraging, but it often gets together in a small group at the warren. Just why these mongooses are so much more solitary than their meerkat cousins is a matter for speculation, but it most probably comes down to habitat. The meerkat forages in open country and so derives safety from numbers and close cooperation

Opposite, above and below *The animated world of the meerkat. These delightful, pixie-like little animals spend their days foraging for the lizards, insects and scorpions that make up the bulk of their diet.*
Right *A yellow mongoose fluffs out its fur against the winter chill.*

within the group. The mongooses on the other hand live largely under cover.

The third species is the banded mongoose, uncommon in the southern Kalahari and first spotted, by a documentary film unit, in 1983. It is rather larger than the others, has a greyish brown coat with a striped pattern, and lives in close-knit packs. It usually scuttles away when threatened but occasionally, like the meerkat, it will resort to collective defence, bristling and growling as it advances en masse towards a jackal or other predator. Remarkably, there have been reports (elsewhere) of banded mongooses actually climbing a tree to rescue a pack-mate taken by an eagle.

THE SKY-DIVERS

Among the most efficient of the desert's daytime predators is the martial eagle, a splendid looking raptor that features prominently among the 52 different birds of prey recorded in the southern Kalahari. The slightly larger female of the species has a 2-metre (2.2-yard) wingspan, weighs around 6 kilograms (13 pounds), and she and her mate cruise a few hundred metres above the ground in search of their prey. Nothing that moves among the dunes or along the river-beds escapes their incredibly sharp eyes: the bird is said to be able to pick out a ground squirrel at a distance of 6 kilometres (3.7 miles). When it spots a

likely meal it planes down in a shallow dive, gaining more and more speed, making the final approach at low altitude so that it remains undetected until the last moment, and then breaks the quarry's body with its sheer weight and momentum. The martial is easily identified, not only by its size and hunting behaviour but also by its distinctively bold markings: dark brown back, wings and chest, and a white front spotted with black dots.

The more common among the region's other eagles include the tawny, whose stick nests can be seen in the trees of the riverbeds; and the imperious blackbreasted snake eagle, largest of all hovering birds of prey and sometimes mistaken for the martial (though it is smaller, and doesn't have black spots on its white front and belly). As its name suggests, the snake eagle preys largely on reptiles, which it hunts either from high in the air (higher than the other eagles), especially on breezy days, or from a lofty perch. When it sights a likely target it will dive or, more usually, parachute down to grasp the snake in its powerful talons and swallow it on the wing.

Above *The martial eagle, largest of the desert's birds of prey.*
Left *A pale chanting goshawk checks the area for danger before drinking. Waterholes are ideal spots for viewing the Kalahari's raptors.*
Opposite, above *The handsome tawny eagle, a resident species.*
Opposite, below *The kori bustard is Africa's heaviest flying bird.*

The southern Kalahari, along with the Kruger, is among the last refuges of the martial and tawny eagles and other large birds of prey. Moreover, because of the open terrain, the clarity of the desert air and the sheer extent of the conservation area, the combined park probably affords better opportunities of viewing them than any other southern African venue.

Richard Liversidge, one-time director of Kimberley's McGregor Museum and a world-renowned ornithologist, has been monitoring the region's raptors for the past two decades and finds that the eagles are, on average, 56 times more common inside the park than outside – a grim indictment of the situation on stockfarming land. Nevertheless, although the combined conservancy is vast it offers relatively few breeding sites (the most favourable habitats are the river-beds and their large trees), so severe limits have been imposed on the number of birds the area can carry. Its maximum capacity, in fact, is reckoned at just 30 martial, 40 tawny and fewer than 20 bateleur pairs, these last (today reduced

to just 11 pairs) found almost exclusively on the upper reaches of the Nossob and the flanking savanna country.

Nor do these species have a particularly good breeding record within the park, largely because climate and food supplies fluctuate so dramatically. Only 50 to 60 per cent of the pairs lay eggs each year, and only half the fledglings survive. In fact, the large-raptor populations have been declining steadily – because they were small to begin with (when a 'vacancy' occurs it is not automatically filled by a new pair); because tourist traffic along the river-beds upsets the birds at nesting time and, not least, because farmers in the surrounding countryside, over which the birds fly on their hunting forays, persecute them. Poison bait left out for jackals and other ground-living carnivores is the biggest killer.

A common enough sight in the southern Kalahari is the secretary bird, a species that enjoys sole membership of its taxonomic family and which usually forages in pairs, though groups of up to 50 can sometimes gather at the boreholes during the hot dry season. Something of an oddity among raptors, the bird lives largely on the ground, striding the sandveld with its head thrust forward, its body rocking from side to side as it hunts the rodents, lizards and occasional snake that comprise its diet – and killing, not with its eagle-like bill but by stamping fast and furiously on the prey. The origin of its curious name is rather obscure: it derives either from the crest, which reminds one vaguely of a row of quill pens tucked behind the ear of an old-fashioned secretary, or, more likely, from the Arabic *saqr-et-tair*, meaning hunter/ hawk-bird.

Harriers, kestrels, hawks, kites, falcons – they're all here, an integral part of the Kalahari scene and a perennial joy to visiting bird enthusiasts. Especially prominent among the smaller raptors are the gabar goshawk, the greater kestrel, the lanner falcon and the pale chanting goshawk, which is easily spotted because it perches in the open (unlike the canopy-preferring gabar) and which, though it feeds on

Left, above and below *The odd-looking secretary bird spends much of its time hunting on the ground. It kills by stamping its prey to death.*

THE AIRBORNE ACROBAT

The bateleur is one of the most striking of all the region's raptors, a predatory species distinguished by its finery – velvet-black head and front, chestnut back, bright red cere, legs and feet – and its short stumpy tail. The latter feature gives it a squat, rather awkward appearance when at rest, but in flight the bird is an essay in delta-winged elegance as it planes along, usually at low altitude and at around 60 kilometres (37 miles) an hour, on an arrow-straight course, its only bodily movement a gentle rocking from side to side. One usually sees it from about 09:00, which for a raptor is a late start but perfectly logical in the context of the bird's physical design and hunting strategy: it is built to glide, keeping aloft by using the small thermals that strengthen as the day heats up. On those rare occasions when the Kalahari is overcast, it remains grounded.

The bateleur's diet encompasses small mammals, birds that find their food on the ground and, especially, small carcasses – which it is extraordinarily adept at locating – and the remains of larger kills. This preference for carrion explains in part the bird's disappearance from South Africa outside the larger conservancies and its serious decline in Zimbabwe and other neighbouring countries. The species has been virtually exterminated south of the Limpopo by the poison bait, usually strychnine, used by stock farmers to keep marauders such as jackals at bay. The crafty jackal has survived well enough, though, while the eagles and other harmless, incidental creatures have been slaughtered to the point of regional extinction.

Bateleur is the French word for acrobat or juggler, and it aptly describes the bird's superb control of the air as it rolls, tumbles and somersaults in its spectacular display flight. It has an unusually lengthy breeding cycle, laying just one egg which it incubates for about eight weeks. The nesting period takes anything from 101 to 194 days. Mother and father share the incubation, brooding and feeding duties.

snakes, lizards and rodents, will often follow and steal food from the honey badger.

Then there are migrants, the steppe eagle and the yellowbilled kites among them, which arrive in numbers during the hot wet season to feast on the sudden proliferations of rodents, termites and other insects *(see also page 71)*. Among the less regular visitors – the vagrants – are such surprising species as pelican and woollynecked stork, African jacana (more closely associated with the great Okavango wetlands), moorhen, crane and paradise flycatcher, all of which depend heavily on an aquatic environment.

SCAVENGERS SUPREME

The most numerous of the park's raptors are the vultures, of which four species are represented: the whitebacked, lappetfaced, Cape and whiteheaded. To the casual observer the vulture, with its scavenger status, long naked neck and frenzied feeding habits, might fall into the 'disgusting' category, but human prejudice must be discounted. The birds play a vital role in the food chain, and in maintaining the fragile ecological balance, acting as the diurnal vacuum cleaners of the African plains, the daytime counterpart of the nocturnal hyaenas. Flying from thermal to thermal a few hundred metres above the ground, they cover enormous distances in search of food. Sometimes they get caught in especially strong upward air currents and are swept far up into the heavens – in one recorded incident a vulture struck a jetliner cruising at 10 000 metres (33 000 feet) above sea level!

Indeed the open sky, with its cool temperatures and promise of safety, serves the vulture much as the burrow serves a rodent. It also acts as a communication medium, a vast theatre in which the players keep a careful watch on each other, quickly homing in when one of their number spots something worth eating. Very little on the ground escapes their attention: the vulture's eyes have twice the magnification of the human's.

Left *Two lappetfaced vultures watch for signs of death. Their immensely strong bills enable them to consume the toughest parts of a carcass.*

It is commonly believed that vultures feed mainly on the remains of carnivore kills, but this is not so: such carcasses make up less than half their diet, the remainder comprising animals that have met non-violent deaths. The majority of these occur in the cold hours of the morning, not too long before the lions, hyaenas and other nocturnal carnivores retire for the day, so the carcasses are usually untouched and available to the birds. Their real competitors are the bacteria and the swarming maggots. During the hot summer months the raptors have no more than a few hours before the invertebrate horde descends (not that this deters them) and other scavengers move in, and it is not long before the carcass is reduced to bone and skin.

So there is always a frenetic, flapping, shrieking scramble to make the most of a rapidly diminishing food source. Whitebacked vultures can fill their crops with 1,5 kilograms (3.3 pounds) of meat within two minutes – and if there are 50 or so of them at the scene, by no means unusual in the Kalahari, a 200-kilogram (440-pound) wildebeest doesn't last long.

While the whitebacks fight over the remains, the larger lappetfaced vultures hover around the edges of the melee, picking at the scraps, waiting their turn, for their greater strength and heavier beaks enable them to tear the skin and sinew denied to their smaller cousins. The whitebacks can often be seen nesting, in smallish colonies of between 15 and 20 pairs, in the handsome camelthorn trees of the upper Nossob river-bed. They are also established around some of the pans. Those at one – the Bayip – suddenly disappeared after many years' residence, the victims in all probability of poisoning: the pan is within easy flying distance of the Namibian farms. By contrast, the lappetfaced vulture is a much shyer species, less gregarious, preferring to nest alone in the smaller trees of the dune country.

THE RARE WILD DOG

One of the most fascinating of Africa's daytime carnivores, though one which is rarely seen in the southern Kalahari, is the wild or Cape hunting dog. During the 1970s a pack, eight individuals in all, settled near the South African park's Twee Rivieren rest-camp. Their numbers fluctuated during the following years, other groups were sighted, but since the mid-1980s there have been few signs of the animals – which is rather strange because the region, with its open terrain and abundant game, would seem an ideal habitat.

Although the species is a member of the dog family Canidae, and despite the superficial resemblance, it is not in fact closely related to the domestic animal. Distinguishing characteristics include its 'tortoise shell' colouring, large round ears and

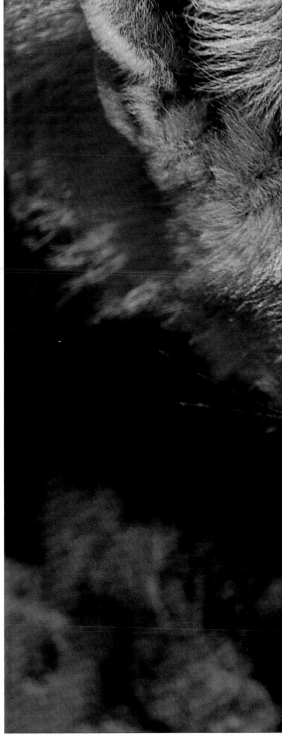

Below *Black-backed jackal in fruitless pursuit of sandgrouse.*
Right *Eating the remains of a springbok.*

white-tipped bushy tail. It is also the only one of the Canidae group to have four and not five toes on its forefoot. It hunts – mainly springbok in the Kalahari (though other small antelope are also taken), impala in the Kruger National Park – by running its prey to exhaustion.

Of all the large predators, the wild dog has perhaps the most intricate, finely balanced social system. Each member of the

pack has its assigned and accepted rank within the group and during the hunt, and its rights to the spoils are subtly and precisely defined. The order of precedence changes over the seasons as the young are born and grow up, adults become old and dominance (the prerogative of the senior female) is challenged. Group survival is the overriding dynamic; all is sacrificed to the wellbeing of the pack as a whole.

Gus Mills, doyen of the southern Kalahari's scientists (though he has latterly transferred to the Kruger), recounts an incident in which six ravenous adults stood back to enable two pups, late arrivals on the scene, to feed first, and points out that the wild dog is the only carnivore that allows its young precedence at the kill. In a poignant variation on this theme another scientist, Allen Reich, recalled the same

unselfish behaviour in the Kruger park. 'All [the animals] were eating peacefully,' he wrote, 'save for the subordinate male. He had made the kill; he had trotted back to the others; he had let them taste the blood on his mouth, and he had led them back to the carcass. Now he waited for what, to our human minds, was rightfully his. He eventually managed a few scraps . . . What a remarkable creature!'

THE NIGHT STALKERS

WHEN DARKNESS FALLS THE DESERT

COMES ALIVE: THE HYAENA AND THE LION

EMERGE FROM THEIR DENS, TO BE JOINED BY

A HOST OF OTHER, SMALLER PREDATORS,

EACH DRIVEN BY THE NEED TO KILL

IN ORDER TO SURVIVE.

Night comes swiftly in the Kalahari. One moment the land is ablaze with the day's last, fiery glow and then, suddenly, the sun is gone, and the red of earth and sky deepens to magenta in the twilight before leaving the world to the starlit darkness. It is now that the desert comes to life, its myriad nocturnal residents, animals large and small, reptiles, birds, insects, emerging into the breeze-blessed coolness to forage for food, to hunt, and to be hunted.

Gus Mills and Michael Knight, two of the park's senior scientists, spent time studying the movements and behaviour of the spotted hyaena – a creature of mystery, the object of superstitious fear and much maligned in fable and myth; in reality a remarkable species, tough, self-sufficient, ingenious, perhaps the most accomplished of the Kalahari's carnivores. Michael Knight recalls a particular evening:

Top *Lions wait for the coming darkness.*
Left *The shy and elusive caracal, present but rarely seen in the Kalahari region.*
Right *Dusk comes to the desert, and one of the Kalahari's large raptors, the giant eagle owl, readies itself for the hunt.*

'We wait and watch, our eyes barely able to make out the hole in the sand crater, once a porcupine's burrow and now home to a family of spotted hyaenas. We know that the adults will come tonight, for there are no fresh tracks and this tells us that they have been away for at least two days, and the youngsters must be ravenous.

'And come they do. A grey ghost appears over the dune crest and makes its way down through the tall grass. This is the matriarch of the clan, the dominant female we call Goldie. She stands over the hole, her head hung low, and gives a deep grunt.

'A small head emerges to peer over the crater's rim, followed by another and then another. The two-month-old cubs catch sight of Goldie and launch into a frantic, ritualized greeting of giggles, raised tails and genital licking before they settle down to suckle. Five minutes later Goldie emits an alarm rumble that sends the cubs scurrying for the burrow. Three other shadows move towards the den, and there is another ceremonial greeting. The newcomers are the mother of the cubs, a sub-adult female and a male who remains slightly apart: he is a member of the clan but

Above *A spotted hyaena at rest near the den-site. This nocturnal animal is both scavenger and hunter, and ranks as the Kalahari's most accomplished opportunist.* **Opposite** *The secretive aardwolf.*

accepted only with reluctance by the matriarch and her close-knit family of daughters, sisters and their progeny.

'We can see from their flat stomachs and clean muzzles that last night's hunt was unsuccessful – a fact that holds promise for the next few hours. And indeed it isn't long

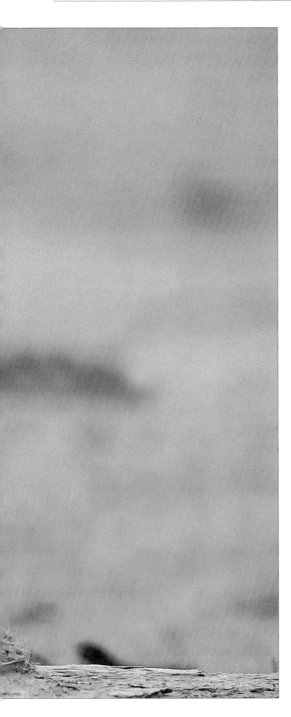

she sets off, leading her retinue, at a fast lope that turns into a 30 kilometre (19 mile) an hour canter, towards the east. To keep in touch with the hunting party we flash the headlights, but sparingly for we know that the illumination could act unfairly against the animals being chased, dazzle them into misjudgement. We cross three dunes before the raised tails, and an increase in pace, tell us that we are closing in on the prey.

'Our view is obscured by a cloud of dust. We are on an open plain and a small group of gemsbok has taken flight, the pack in pursuit, manoeuvering to single out one of the calves. The hyaenas are weaving among and around the galloping herd, and when two of the gemsbok, a cow and a calf, break away they veer off to follow them. After about a kilometre the quarry begins to tire and circle back, allowing the hyaenas to gain on them. The bigger gemsbok stops to fight it out and is ignored; the gasping calf runs on and the pack, sensing success, chase it for another 200 metres (220 yards) until they are within striking distance. They tear at its rump and sides, and then pull it down. It gives a few weak kicks, makes a desperate attempt to rise, and then it dies.

'The hyaenas tear at the carcass, feeding voraciously, snapping and giggling in their ravenous frenzy. Twenty minutes later they are satiated, red from the kill, and the male hyaena whoops into the silent night to signal success. Goldie sets off, before the carcass is finished and before her food is digested, back towards the den and the waiting cubs.'

THE WORLD OF THE HYAENA

The Kalahari is home to two hyaena species, the spotted and the brown, together with the related aardwolf (see page 78). The spotted is the largest of the three, females weighing in at around 75 kilograms, (165 pounds) the males somewhat less. Clans number up to 15 or so individuals, most of them closely related females and their cubs. The few males in the group have subservient status.

Popular myth holds that hyaenas are hermaphrodites, a misconception that stems from the female's prominent male-like sexual organs. These, in both the sexes, are central to the greeting ceremony: the animals stand head to tail and lift their hind legs, so presenting their most vulnerable parts to the other's lethal jaws. The ritual has no sexual connotation; it is simply a demonstration of mutual trust, reaffirming clan loyalties and cementing the ties between members of an extended family.

The heart of the hyaena community is the den, though often the animals don't construct one for themselves but simply take over a ready-made burrow, usually built by an aardvark and later enlarged by porcupines. The den, invariably a burrow with a spacious entrance that narrows into a tunnel, provides the cubs – who spend a lot of time on their own while the adults are out seeking food – with security from lions, jackals and other predators. It is also the hub of the clan's social life and, moreover, serves as a kind of information centre, a gathering place where clan members maintain contact with each other, establish their status within the group, learn about feeding prospects. But communal living does have its drawbacks: closeness in a confined space provokes infestations of parasites, notably fleas, that accumulate to become a real irritant. So, once every two months or so, the clan moves on to find another den.

The clan is a flexible unit, its membership fluctuating in size and composition from week to week. Close relatives usually stay together but other individuals come

before Goldie and the other two females rise and move off into the darkness, the male a little to the rear. Our old diesel truck kicks into life and, with only the orange parking lights shining, we follow them, at a discreet distance, up the dune towards the silver ribbon in the distance, the Nossob river-bed.

'The hyaenas reach the river, halt briefly to lap at the waterhole and then turn south, alternatively loping and walking. After some five kilometres Goldie stops, sniffs the ground and the air, her head held high, tail curved upwards, and suddenly

and go as the mood takes them and as feeding opportunities occur. For hyaenas are opportunists *par excellence*. As we have seen, they are not, contrary to popular belief, simply the supreme scavengers of the African veld but also among the most resourceful of its hunters. Gus Mills has found that, in the southern Kalahari, they kill 60 per cent of their food – about the same rate as their cousins in East Africa but far higher than that in the Kruger National Park, where the terrain is more densely vegetated. The freshness of the food is an important factor in the desert for it provides much-needed moisture, in a largely waterless region, as well as sustenance.

The clans, of which there are ten (80 to 100 individuals in total) in the South African park, tend to favour gemsbok and wildebeest but take a whole array of smaller prey down to mice and birds. The adult antelope, naturally, are the most difficult to kill – especially the gemsbok, which can wield their sharp horns with deadly force and accuracy – but the hyaenas usually test the field with a preliminary chase, stampeding the herd to expose the weaker, more vulnerable, animals.

Spotted hyaenas do scavenge, of course, though the kills of other carnivores account for a surprisingly small part of the total food intake. Most of the carcasses are those of animals that have died from non-violent causes, of disease or starvation. These the hyaenas locate with almost uncanny precision, guided to the spot by their superb sense of smell. Special, too, is the strength of their jaws and teeth, features powerful enough to crush the bones for the rich marrow they contain. Their digestive systems are also incredibly tough, able to process the bones themselves.

Resourcefulness, together with flexibility and intra-clan cooperation, are the keys to the spotted hyaena's success. A pack, for instance, can actually rob lions of a kill, harassing and mobbing their much larger and more powerful rivals until the latter

Left *Lean pickings – a spotted hyaena chews with powerful jaws on the last remains of a steenbok carcass.*
Opposite *As darkness approaches, spotted hyaena set out for the hunt in the Kwang Pan area.*

MARKING OUT THE HOME RANGE

Hyaenas and their aardwolf relatives are strictly territorial animals, though they don't patrol their borders. Instead they scent-mark the area with a special paste produced by sacs sited between the rectum and the tail. The brown hyaena (right) operates the most elaborate of the pasting systems, first depositing a creamy white secretion on grass stalks and then, just above this, a black substance. It repeats the procedure every 300 metres (328 yards) or so, which – if its foraging expedition extends over, say, 30 kilometres (19 miles) – adds up to something approaching 600 pastings each night. And the odour lasts a full month, during which time its territory could embrace a prodigious 18 000 active scent-marks – a formidable barrage of smells to warn off would-be intruders. The scent, still detectable by humans a month after being deposited (imagine then the effect it has on the infinitely more sensitive wildlife!), tells other hyaenas which group has rights to the territory, which individual has passed that way and how long ago. In this way neighbouring clans (though largely solitary, brown hyaenas do live in loose associations) avoid encroaching on each other's turf, and members of the same group do not waste time foraging in an area already exploited. Spotted hyaenas also scent-mark but far less frequently (one pasting every three to eight kilometres), and mainly to identify a territory rather than to leave specific messages for other

foragers. For person-to-person communication they rely on the characteristic whoop, a signal that identifies their location and informs other group members of a carcass or likely kill, or of the presence of their mortal enemy, the lion. Aardwolves are the champion scent-markers, placing up to 20 secretions per kilometre to mark their comparatively small territories with as many as 100 000 pastings each month.

retire with what dignity they can muster. Indeed there are recorded incidents, in the Kalahari and elsewhere, of a lion being chased up a tree and kept there, in terror, by a determined hyaena pack. This hostility between the two very different species seems to go beyond the immediate struggle for a particular carcass: there is an element of deliberate and sustained mutual antagonism that probably derives from a dependence on the same food items. In an area with very finite resources, they are obliged to compete head-on.

All this hyaena activity is invariably accompanied by an array of the most bizarre sounds. The animal has an impressive and unearthly vocal repertoire that includes loud whoops, shrieks, giggles, maniacal laughter, calls that chill the heart on moonlit nights and feed the legends in which it is wreathed. To rural people throughout Africa hyaenas are the pack-horses of witches, the bringers of death, the embodiment of evil. The truth is a lot more prosaic but, to students of the wild, just as fascinating.

Much less prominent are the Kalahari's brown hyaenas. Unlike their spotted cousins they are solitary foragers (though

they do associate in loose clans within well-marked territories; *see box page 105*), silent for the most part, seldom hunting for their food (they will, however, take small mammals such as springhares, springbok lambs and bateared foxes), depending rather on kills made by other predators and on a fairly extensive menu that includes beetles, termites, mice and, for water as well as food, tsamma melons and gemsbok cucumbers. They also relish ostrich eggs, highly nutritious items which they are able to bite through. Here they hold a distinct advantage over the spotteds, which cannot get their mouths around the eggs and so resort to rolling them against each other to break them open.

Both species, but more notably the brown hyaena, are prodigious hoarders of man-made objects: a visit to the latter's den will invariably reveal a bizarre collection of tin cans, mugs, old shoes and other pieces of human detritus, material scavenged on the open veld and often in the precincts of the rest-camps themselves. The animals are notorious, in fact, for their ability to infiltrate and burgle camps, especially those safari venues where visitors live under canvas and security is often minimal. Few bush larders, fridges and meat-safes are impervious to their ingenuity and their steel-like jaws.

CATS OF THE DESERT

Few sights can be as memorable as a magnificent Kalahari lion, perhaps one of those with a black mane, standing atop a red dune surveying his vast domain. He is the largest of the desert predators and, though essentially nocturnal, can often be spotted during the daytime.

The South African section of the combined park is haven to between 110 and 180 lions distributed among ten prides – a population that is probably kept artificially high by the man-made waterholes and the many herbivores they sustain. Never-

Left, above *A Cape fox pup investigates a giant millipede, and will soon retreat: these huge insects secrete a highly toxic substance when threatened.*
Left *This lioness is pirating her meal – the springbok was killed by a cheetah.*
Opposite *Resting after the night's kill.*

theless, the region's vegetation is scattered, sporadic and sparse, the density of the prey animals is low and the lions roam across enormous home ranges – more than 400 square kilometres (150 miles²) in extent, 16 times larger than those in the better-watered Kruger National Park.

These lion communities, the southern Kalahari's and the Kruger's, have a unique and cherished place on the South African wildlife scene, for they are the country's only two viable populations of the species. It was not always so. Long ago, before man and his cattle changed the face of the land, these great carnivores hunted the region in numbers, but the herds have long since disappeared and the occasional cat that does wander outside the conservancy's boundaries is ruthlessly persecuted. Recently the pride that lived in the park's Mata Mata area strayed onto an adjacent

Namibian farm and killed a few goats, for which mild transgression almost every member of the group was shot to death. The loss of these animals, from a smallish population of around 70 adults, could have a devastating impact on the gene pool – and thus on the survival of the species in the southern Kalahari. Less genetic exchange between the various prides will eventually reduce each one's ability to adapt, to cope with environmental change.

Although majestic in appearance and supremely dominant in their strength and hunting prowess, lions prey on the smaller animals – steenbok, foxes, aardvarks, springhares and so on – to a far greater extent in the Kalahari than elsewhere. The humble porcupine, for instance, accounts for a surprising 32 per cent of the kills, an average figure that reflects food intake during the long droughts, periods when

the land is dry and game is scarce. Antelope are the Kalahari's preferred prey in times of plenty. The older and weaker animals tend to be targeted, and oddly enough a greater number of males than females are taken – which indicates that solitary, territorial bulls and rams (which have only their own senses to warn them) are always more vulnerable than a group of mothers and calves.

Lions have no natural enemies, but the mortality rate among the prides is unexpectedly high, the heaviest toll taken by starvation among the cubs during the lean seasons, by the aggression of adult males, and by parasite-born diseases that attack the young when they are in poor condition. Moreover, the porcupine is not as harmless a prey animal as it seems: its needle-sharp quills can pierce the flesh to set up a debilitating infection that will eventually weaken

the cat so that it can no longer hunt. Happily, though, this is a rare occurrence; the quills are usually pulled out or they simply drop off.

Lions are the only members of the cat family to live in groups, a system that confers a number of distinct advantages. Lionesses that team up, for example, are better able to protect their cubs from males that take over the pride. And, more importantly, they can hunt more efficiently in a team. The cooperative effort is especially effective when the prey is a particularly large animal such as a gemsbok bull or (elsewhere) a buffalo. An increase in the number of hunters from one to a group of, say, three will increase the rate of successful kills by 20 per cent. Moreover, cooperative animals are better able to defend their territories than such solitary species as leopards and cheetahs.

Group living also has benefits when it comes to raising the young. The cubs have more adults to protect them, and closely related females will suckle each other's offspring when the mothers are, for one reason or another, away from the pride.

Smaller but in its own way just as handsome, indeed beautiful, is the leopard, perhaps the most adaptable and resilient of all the bigger predators. The species has an especially wide distribution, occurring from the southern tip of Africa right up the continent and across to eastern Asia, its habitats varying from high mountain to coastal region and from lush equatorial forest to desert.

It is also the only large carnivore to survive, if not to thrive, outside game parks and other protected areas, though in the southern African region its numbers have been drastically reduced by urban sprawl and the development of the interior farmlands. Nevertheless this predator remains elusive and wily enough to sidestep human encroachment, and now and again it turns up in some pretty unexpected places – on the outskirts of cities such as Cape Town, Johannesburg and other major

centres, for instance, and even in the gardens of some rural homesteads and the precincts of park rest-camps.

The chief reason for the leopard's outstanding success is its varied diet: it will take more or less any warm-blooded animal prey, ranging from a tiny mouse up to the sturdy hartebeest. It will often haul the bigger prey into a tree – a masterly stratagem for keeping its meal safe from marauding hyaenas, and from vultures wheeling in the sky above, which cannot see through the canopy and do not perch to feed. Essentially, though, the leopard is not an arboreal species: it spends most of

its time on terra firma, only taking to trees to escape its predators, notably lions, and to cache its food.

For the rest, the leopard is very much a solitary creature of the night. Males and females live apart; the male, which is much the larger of the two – 60 as against 40 kilograms (132 as against 88 pounds) in body weight – has an extensive territory that normally overlaps with those of several female leopards. The female gives birth to between one and three cubs. When her offspring are about a year old, she becomes increasingly impatient, even aggressive with them, comes into oestrus

Opposite and right *Although a mainly nocturnal predator, the handsome and highly adaptable leopard does venture abroad on cool, overcast days. This particular specimen, from the Twee Rivieren area, is an especially expert hunter.*

and begins scent-marking and calling to attract a new mate. The young are then unceremoniously evicted.

Next in descending order of size among the cats is the caracal, also known as the *rooikat* (Afrikaans) and the lynx (but not to be confused with its European and North American namesake), an attractive animal with tufted ears and handsome reddish coat. And fierce it is, too, the embodiment of fury as it spits and hisses defiance at the jackals that hover at mealtimes. It hunts by stalking its prey – the smaller antelope, springhares, rodents – until it gets within a few metres, and then pounces with lightning speed. It also feeds on birds, catching them on the ground, in their nests and, remarkably, on the wing: its immensely powerful hind limbs enable it to leap several metres into the air.

Finally there is the African wild cat, roughly the same size and barely distin-

guishable from the domestic tabby. Indeed the species is the common ancestor, first domesticated more than 3 000 years ago in Pharaonic Egypt. You can, though, tell them apart if you look at the backs of their ears: the former's are reddish brown, the latter's black or dark brown. The wild cat is also heavier, its legs slightly longer, its build heavier. The two do interbreed, which has corrupted the wild variety's gene pool in all but the remotest areas. The species has a catholic diet: mice and rats are favoured, of course, but it will catch anything from a springhare down to lizards, small birds and even locusts.

JACKALS, FOXES AND OTHERS

The grand master of the Kalahari's opportunists, though, is neither the brown hyaena nor the leopard – impressively adaptable as they are – but the attractive black-

Above *The small-spotted genet, a strictly night-time and for the most part solitary little carnivore, feeds on insects, geckos and other lizards, and on wild fruits.*
Opposite *The black-backed jackal is ground-living but occasionally climbs a tree in search of the remains of a carcass carried up by a leopard.*

backed jackal. This versatile animal is both hunter and scavenger, active by day as well as night, and will eat just about anything that moves and much that doesn't: rodents, springhares, locusts, termites and other insects, birds' eggs and fledglings, reptiles, carrion, and even wild plants. Sometimes it functions on its own; at others – in periods of severe drought, for example, when antelope mortality is often high – it comes together in groups of 20 or 30 animals to demolish a carcass.

These little creatures, in fact, are surprisingly brave and tenacious at kills made by the larger predators, nipping at the heels of spotted hyaenas and lions, hurrying them along in order to gain access to the carcass that much sooner. They will even take part in kills in the making: jackals have been observed following a cheetah as it stalks an antelope herd. And during the springbok lambing season, in an apparent departure from the social norm, they will operate in small packs, one member of which distracts the mother while the others isolate and bring down her calf. They also tend to pick out the old and weak from the herd, and in so doing play a significant part in maintaining the balance in, and the health of their ecosystem. This food source, however, is supplementary rather than basic to their diet.

Black-backed jackals are a monogamous species, pairing up and producing three to four pups each season. The family usually disperses once the young can fend for themselves, but occasionally one or more

stay on to help nurture the next litter. One of the mysteries surrounding the animal, in fact, is its breeding period: the pups are born in winter and early spring, which is a barren time on the sandveld – the rodents and insects which comprise the jackal's staple diet are in short supply. Just why this extraordinarily adaptable species hasn't evolved to give birth in more favourable circumstances is a matter for some speculation. Breeding does, though, coincide with the advent of the springbok lambs (in good years), and with the drought that causes starvation and a relatively high mortality rate among the herds. So the pack-hunt might not be the sporadic, opportunistic event that the received wisdom says it is but, instead, an essential part of the jackal biology.

Left and right *Springhares emerge well after dark. Their burrows comprise a single resting chamber with up to 11 escape exits.*
Below *Barking geckos, whose 'tapping' call is an evocative sound of a warm Kalahari summer's evening.*

Above *In the Kalahari the lethally venomous* Parabuthus *scorpion is especially active on hot, windy nights.*
Left *The honey badger – a shy and retiring animal despite its fierce reputation. It is, though, armed with sharp teeth and even sharper claws, and will confront a threat with courage.*
Opposite *Kalahari moonrise.*

A second and related enigma involves the species' social system. Essentially, as noted, the family appears to be the basic unit, the pack an occasional and random association. Yet the jackal, like the wholly cooperative spotted hyaena and wild dog, boasts a complex range of social skills, and a rank structure which predetermines dominance and submissiveness. Again, it may be that the widely held assumptions are flawed. The ecologist Andrew McKenzie suggests a new interpretation. 'Could it be', he asks, 'that the large groups of jackals seen at kills and carcasses, and the mobbing call that alerts other jackals to

the presence of a larger predator, represent the true jackal social system – a 'cryptic' pack that communicates and cooperates whenever necessary but which, for the rest of the time, pretends to be a collection of small, separate family groups?'

The southern Kalahari is home to two types of fox, the larger and more common of which is the bat-eared species *Otocyon megalotis*, an enchanting little animal distinguished by its bushy black tail, rounded back and, its most prominent feature, enormous dish-like ears. These last it uses as supersensitive sound amplifiers to locate the harvester termites and beetle larvae that comprise its favoured food. The ears are held forward as it listens for the faint sounds of its prey beneath the surface of the sandveld – the insects stand little chance of avoiding detection, even at night. The fox also eats a fair selection of other creatures, including small rodents, scorpions, locusts, adult beetles and certain desert plants. Like the jackal it is monogamous: the pair usually remain together for their entire adult lives and share the parenting duties. The mother fulfils most of the foraging while, for much of the time, the father guards the den and its young occupants.

Generally similar in habit and habitat but smaller and arguably even more attractive is the petite Cape or silver fox *Vulpes chama*, just 3 kilograms (6.6 pounds) in weight and southern Africa's only true fox. It too has large ears but the first thing you notice is its tail, an enormous bushy affair more than a third as long as its body. The appendage is not merely decorative, though: like everything else in the natural world it has evolved for a reason, in this instance helping balance the little animal in its weaving, twisting flight from predators. It also serves as a decoy, drawing the hunter's eyes (and claws) away from the body – hence the Afrikaans name *draaijakkals*, or 'turning jackal'.

Darkness in the Kalahari mantles a myriad other animals, creatures that hide away in the hot hours and emerge to hunt and forage in the coolness of the night. Among the larger and, when cornered, fiercer ones is the honey badger or ratel, a sturdy, coarse-coated mustelid. As its name suggests, it is partial to honey, seeking out and ripping apart beehives with its long, powerful, knife-like claws. But this seems to be

a rare food source in the desert. Most of the animal's intake comprises prey of one kind or another – beetles, scorpions, small rodents and reptiles – which it digs out of the ground. Other sandveld residents, notably chanting goshawks and the occasional jackal, often accompany the badger on its digging expeditions, gobbling up escapees from the excavations.

The honey badger, despite its reputation for aggressiveness, is a generally shy animal and will retire into its hole when disturbed. But it has plenty of courage and, if it cannot retreat, will confront a threat with bared teeth, snarling defiance, sometimes charging its persecutor. Occasionally, too, it will rob prey from a larger carnivore.

The second of the southern Kalahari's mustelids, the striped polecat, is a much smaller (it weighs less than a kilogram or 2 pounds) and more distinctively marked animal: it has four white stripes along its black back, white patches between eyes and ears, a white spot on its forehead and a long bushy white tail which it raises

Left *Spotted eagle owl chicks, who were born in relays, await the return of their food-bearing parents.*
Above *Mottled grey coloration and ear-tufts serve as excellent daytime camouflage for the spotted eagle owl.*
Opposite, above *A relaxed but ever-alert gemsbok bull reflectively chews its cud.*
Opposite, below *This bat-eared fox is listening for the underground movement of its insect prey.*

when alarmed – a prelude to releasing its miasmic protective smell. This species, an insectivore, is wholly nocturnal.

The desert night also has its airborne predators: the region embraces six species of resident owl (and one occasional visitor), ranging from the 2-kilogram (4.4-pound) giant eagle owl down to the diminutive scops. Visitors to the South African park's Nossob rest-camp, an especially favoured spot, can see or, more usually, hear up to four different species on a warm summer's night. The most common of them is the whitefaced, which during the periodic explosive rodent booms are so satiated that they litter the area with the corpses of uneaten rats and mice. In such generous times a pair of these owls can produce three clutches from which three young are usually raised. Other species include the barn and the pearlspotted owls.

SEEDS OF LIFE

THE ANIMALS AND PLANTS

OF THE KALAHARI SURVIVE, AS SPECIES,

BECAUSE THEY EXTRACT THE MAXIMUM ADVANTAGE

FROM THOSE FEW, ALL-TOO-BRIEF TIMES WHEN

THE ENVIRONMENT IS FAVOURABLE

FOR REPRODUCTION.

One of the more remarkable members of the southern Kalahari's modest floral community is *Harpagophytum procumbens*, or the grapple-thorn, informally known as 'devil's claw'. A resident of the dunelands, it belongs to the melon family (though you wouldn't think so to look at it), and its subterranean tuber sends out long tendrils equipped with seed pods and wicked little grapple hooks that will snag and cling to the hoof of a passing antelope. In due course the pods will be crushed underfoot and their seeds scattered over the sandveld. The hooks, though, remain embedded and can set up a sometimes fatal infection. Occasionally the claw will fasten onto a browsing animal's mouth and eventually kill it by slow starvation.

The grapple-thorn's seed dispersal strategy is one example, albeit a particularly enterprising one, of the many ways in which the region's plants have adapted to the rigours of climate and terrain.

Top *Lion cub in relaxed mode.*
Left *A gemsbok bull displays the 'flehmen' grimace – behaviour that is designed to detect whether the female is ready to mate.*
Right *The strange 'devil's claw' plant.*

ANNUALS AND PERENNIALS

All organisms, everywhere, invest heavily in the business of propagation, but desert conditions – temperature extremes, lack of moisture, uncertain rains – present special difficulties, which have prompted an array of adaptations among plants and animals that are fascinating in their ingenuity and variety. At base, though, the processes come down to just two imperatives: the need to optimize progeny output to ensure the long-term species survival and, within that framework, to extract maximum advantage from those unpredictable and all-too-brief periods when the environment is favourable for reproduction.

The Kalahari's annual plants are masterly opportunists. During the long droughts their seeds lie dormant on or just beneath the ground for months and sometimes for years until conditions are just right, at which point they germinate and flower in a matter of days (*see page 53*). Seed dispersal follows shortly afterwards.

Annuals are the foremost colonizers of the desert, the first plants to establish themselves on new ground. Some rely on the wind for pollination – very much of a hit-or-miss option, and an expensive one in terms of energy: huge amounts of light-weight pollen, invariably of a wing-like design suitable for 'parachute' distribution, must be produced without any guarantee that it will carry to and fertilize the eggs of the same species in far-off places. And, of course, a high proportion of the randomly scattered seeds are eaten by insects and rodents. The seeds of other annuals are borne away by animals – by the butterflies, beetles, bees and other invertebrates of the desert – which are a lot more reliable and economic than the wind because they carry pollen directly from one plant to another, and because flowering is

Opposite *An attractive little Cape fox and her pup. The handsome bushy tails of these carnivores – a third as long as their bodies – help balance the animals in their weaving, twisting flight from predators.* **Right** *The 'devil's claw' in flower (see page 119). Like many other tough plants of the Kalahari this species has evolved ingenious methods of seed dispersal.*

synchronized with their emergence in numbers. But then rivalry for their attention is inevitably intense, stimulating the production of an eye-catching variety of flower shapes and colours.

Some desert plants, notably those of the Asteraceae family that is especially prominent farther to the southwest of the southern Kalahari – annuals that illuminate the sandy plains of Namaqualand in springtime with their daisy-like flowers – produce two (and occasionally even three) types of seed, each wind-blown in a different way. One type is structured to fall close by in order to share the parent plant's patch with its proven nurturing capacity; the other is designed to be carried further away to pioneer new habitats.

An intriguing feature of some annuals is their delayed-action adaptive approach to the briefness and unpredictability of the desert rains. For these short-lived species to depend on a single shower, which could yield too little moisture and may be followed by a drought that lasts for months or even years, is to invite disaster. Mass-germination would, almost literally, consign all their eggs to one basket. They counter the threat by staggering the process, bearing different seeds that, to a greater or lesser degree, will bide their time, some germinating during the current rains, others next season, still others several seasons down the line. Their secret: a special substance, occurring in different amounts within the seeds, that stops germination but which is progressively leached out by the rain. Thus those seeds with smaller amounts of the chemical germinate at an early stage, while those with the higher concentrations wait for the second, fifth or even tenth downpour to release their life force. And so the plants spread the risks, ensuring that a high percentage of their progeny will survive the vagaries of the desert climate.

The large perennials of the southern Kalahari are not nearly so vulnerable to drought, because they put down long taproots that soak up water from deep beneath the surface. Unlike the annuals, they are not opportunists: they do not need a special cue – notably the promise or onset of rain – to trigger the reproductive cycle but instead tend to follow, be part of, the seasonal rhythms, drawing upon reserves stored in their roots from the last rains that fell.

The seeds of some Kalahari tree species are distributed by the wind, but a high proportion – unusually high compared with the tree populations of less arid regions – depend on insects, and on vertebrates of one kind or another. The hardy and handsome camelthorn produces relatively few seeds but the pods are big, rich in protein and highly attractive to gemsbok and eland. And they are also ingeniously designed along delayed-action lines: each pod is covered in an extremely hard 'tunic' that protects the nutritious pulp in which the seeds are embedded, acting as an airtight, watertight casing (which enables it to remain in the ground for long periods) that is virtually impervious to the powerful grinding of herbivore teeth (though not to the parasitical Bruchid seed-eating beetles).

When they are swallowed, however, they are softened by the animal's digestive acids and, once they pass out in the faeces, become susceptible to moisture and germinate with the first rain.

As in nearly every other evolutionary association, the relationship between browsing animals and plants is exquisitely designed to benefit both parties. The browsers get their food, and in return distribute the seeds over an extensive area – especially extensive in the Kalahari, where ungulates range widely to obtain their daily intake. Moreover, the seeds are invariably passed out in a place favourable for growth since the animal and the parent tree share the same habitat. Growth prospects are improved even further by the nutrient-rich dung in which the pods are deposited.

A few desert trees compete for insect pollinators, offering them an abundance of pollen and nectar. The smelly shepherd's tree *Boscia foetida* (an uncommon resident of the southern Kalahari) is especially distinctive in its enticement: its flowers are pungent with the foul odour of excrement. Other trees of the wider region, notably those of the subfamily Stapelieae (and notably *Stapelia barklyi*), give off the smell of rotting meat.

Breeding and growth patterns among the invertebrates are complex. Insect eggs vary greatly from species to species in their sizes, shapes and numbers. In some, the eggs remain inside the body until they hatch, and the young are born live. The transition to adulthood is then negotiated in stages, in a series of 'moults' as the exoskeleton, or outer shell (which is incapable of expansion), is replaced.

Among the termites, dragonflies, stick insects, grasshoppers, locusts, bugs, lice and others, the hatchlings or 'nymphs' are similar to the adults in all respects except size, and the transition from young to adult is relatively simple. In other species, however – butterflies, beetles, wasps, bees, ants – there is what is known as 'complete metamorphosis', a sequence in which the young hatch into larvae that look nothing like their parents. After a number of moults, they change into pupae, which is the intermediate stage: pupae resemble neither the larva nor the adult, and are often encased in a cocoon within which further structural changes occur before the final product emerges.

The subject is enormously complicated, but it is worth touching on one or two of the region's more prominent species.

The dung beetle is very much part of the Kalahari scene. In fact it's a ubiquitous creature that belongs to the enormously varied Scarabaeidae family that embraces about 4 000 different species world-wide, of which some 2 000 are endemic to Africa and nearly 800 to the southern subcontinent. Some are tiny; others can reach a full 6 centimetres (2,3 inches) in length; all are masterly scavengers, the vacuum cleaners of the veld. Their efficiency at finding and removing mammal droppings is quite amazing: the insects converge, sometimes in great numbers (more than 7 000 have been observed at one pile of elephant dung in the Kruger National Park), almost

Left *A scorpion falls victim to a yellow-billed hornbill, a meal which will be offered to his mate who is sealed into the nest while laying and incubating the eggs.*
Opposite, top *The everpresent dung beetle, the most efficient, and valuable, of the desert's scavengers.*

before the animal has completed its bowel movement, and remove the waste in double-quick time. In the process they help control the spread of harmful bacteria and other disease vectors, and destroy the eggs of parasites that, left intact, will find their way into and damage the intestines of herbivores. By carrying away the dung, too, the beetles distribute natural fertilizer, returning precious faecal nitrogen to the soil.

All dung beetles use animal droppings as their prime food source – for themselves and for their larvae. Some species lay their eggs beneath the dung-pat, others inside the pat, and still others – the *Scarabaeus* species (among them the sacred scarab of ancient Egypt) – model a large piece, up to 40 times the insect's own mass, into a ball and, using their back legs and their fast-moving wings for propulsion, roll it away and bury it a few centimetres beneath the surface. There, the male and female mate, and feed on the dung cache, after which they prepare a 'brood-ball'. The female dung beetle smooths the latter to

a perfect roundness, makes a hole in its side and deposits a single egg. She then covers up the hole's entrance and moves off to repeat the process elsewhere. When the egg hatches the grub eats the inside of the ball, whose outer surface hardens to form a protective casing.

Another invertebrate that also merits mention for its distinctive breeding habits

is the scorpion, renowned for its 'mating dance'. This is not, however, the light-hearted affair it sounds like, but a highly functional behavioural sequence, designed to clear the ground of obstacles prior to copulation, in which the male grasps his partner's pincers and pushes and pulls her, the to-and-fro movement smoothing the soil underfoot. He then deposits his sperm sack on the cleared patch and manoeuvres her over it so that she can draw up the sperm. The young develop in a pouch inside her body and are born live, scrambling up onto their mother's back soon after they emerge. Scorpions are excellent parents, which is unusual in the world of arthropods: the offspring remain with and are protected by the mother until they reach maturity, which can take several seasons. Oddly enough, although the mothers are endearingly attentive towards their young, cannibalism forms a major part of their diet. These arachnids have a remarkably long lifespan, some species living for up to 30 years.

THE MAMMAL THAT LIVES LIKE AN INSECT

One of the most extraordinary creatures of the desert is the Damara mole-rat, a species whose organization and behaviour resemble nothing so much as those of the social insects. The species, like the ants, bees and termites and quite unlike any other mammal, is in fact 'eusocial', living in underground burrows that are virtually sealed from the surface in colonies of up to 40 individuals. Each colony has its queen, its workers and an elite minority of sturdy soldiers.

Only the queen mole-rat will breed and, to do so, makes sure that the other, smaller females are unable to do so: the eggs in their ovaries remain undeveloped and they are not receptive to mating. On the death of the queen, however, several of these females begin putting on weight before battling each other for succession to the throne.

Unlike the eusocial insects, however, the mole-rats do not disperse in order to establish new colonies: the non-breeding females come to terms with their repressed state and stay with the group. This is surprising when one considers how powerful the reproductive drive is throughout the natural world, but in the desert there are even stronger imperatives. Food is scarce for all its residents, and the mole-rat faces special disadvantages: it forages for geophytic plants beneath the surface of the sandveld in a necessarily random fashion – in this environment, sight and smell are useless, food is found by chance, and the colony needs to keep up its numbers if it is to locate enough plants to survive as a viable entity. In a word, it simply cannot afford to lose members through dispersal.

Which means, of course, that mothers must mate with their sons, thus breaking one of the animal world's most widely held taboos. Inbreeding tends to corrupt the gene pool, allowing recessive genes to mingle and create abnormalities. However, in the fast-breeding mole-rat community defective members usually die early (so eliminating the faulty genes) without making a noticeable impact on the size of the colony. Moreover, with constant inbreeding over the generations, every member of the community is closely related to every other member, so the passing on of one's genes – the prime urge of all organisms – is assured: as long as the queen produces cubs, each individual is guaranteed immortality.

THE GENES IMPERATIVE

Most vertebrates (humankind being a notable exception) breed according to a calendar, the precise timing dictated by an environmental trigger associated with weather and the 'photoperiod' – basically, the number of hours of daylight and darkness. These conditions change with the coming and going of the seasons, and at the optimum point, established aeons ago by the evolutionary processes, the animal's glands will respond, releasing the correct amount of the hormone melatonin to begin the reproductive cycle.

This is what is known as the 'primary cue', and it presupposes a certain regularity in the seasons and their weather patterns, a certainty that at approximately the same time each year circumstances will be favourable for breeding. But consistency is not a feature of the Kalahari: the rains are uncertain, random in their distribution in time and space, food supplies unreliable. Thus much of the desert's wildlife reacts opportunistically to secondary cues – to a good downpour, for instance, or marked changes in the volume and nutritional value of food items, to temperature fluctuation and so forth.

Some rodent species respond dramatically to rain, producing litter after litter, while the bonanza lasts, to create the population explosions that are such a feature of desert life (others, however – the black-tailed rat, for example – are governed solely by the primary cue, the day-night

Left *Food for the young – a spotted hyaena has deposited the remains of a gemsbok calf in its den.*
Below *Whistling rat pups clinging to their mother's fur.*

photoperiod, and give birth regularly throughout the year). Many of the Kalahari's birds are also opportunistic breeders, taking advantage of the plant and insect life that burgeons with the coming of rain. Among these are the sociable weavers *(see page 72)*, which will breed immediately after a good shower of 20 millimetres (0.8 inches) or more and at any time of the year (they are well protected, by their huge, insulated nest complexes, from the stresses of extreme heat and cold). Unusually, the first-born chicks stay on after they mature to help nurture the later offspring, which considerably enhances their chances of survival at the tail end of the insect boom.

Another social mammal with unusual altruistic breeding habits is the meerkat or suricate *(see page 149)*, whose young are born in summer. When the dominant female gives birth, one of the subadult females stays behind to look after the

Above, and following page *For the meerkat, the welfare of the group is the driving force; breeding members are given special privileges.*
Left *A male yellowbilled hornbill feeds his mate, encased in her nest.*

offspring (a vital task in an environment where snakes, birds of prey and other predators pose a constant threat) while the rest of the group venture out to look for food. The mother goes out with them and is allowed to forage without interruption – she is excused sentry duty – in order to build up her milk supplies. This kind of selfless behaviour is unusual among mammals but, again, subadult meerkats – both those that stay behind and the sentries that stand guard over the foraging group – have close blood-ties with all their fellow members, so there is a gene-driven vested interest in ensuring the welfare of

the group as a whole and its capacity to propagate. Subadult female meerkats do occasionally produce their own litters, though in these instances the matriarch usually kills the young.

BOVID BREEDING PATTERNS

The Kalahari's antelope are, for the most part, far less opportunistic breeders than the smaller mammals of the sandveld: they cannot respond quickly to environmental cues – to sudden rainfall and the food it brings – simply because their gestation periods are too long. Their reproductive cycles are geared to the seasons.

Wildebeest, red hartebeest and springbok are territorial animals, the stronger males of each species establishing their personal fiefdoms and retaining all females that happen to be on that particular patch or who subsequently wander in. These the

males guard assiduously, putting an enormous amount of effort into keeping out would-be rivals – so much so that they often don't have time to feed properly and thus suffer a degree of physical deterioration. Moreover, they tend to remain in their territories outside the breeding period,

Previous page, above *Springbok lamb suckling; in good rainfall years two broods may be produced.* **Below** *Wildebeest mother and her calf.*
Left *Red hartebeest infant calves are hidden from predators until strong enough to join the herd.*
Below *A wildebeest bull makes sure the wandering cow stays in his territory.*
Opposite *Springbok fight for dominance in the Auob River valley.*

even when the dry land offers little sustenance, in order to make sure of their turf for the following season (hence the popular misconception that the lone animals one sees are old bulls rejected by the herd). In these circumstances they are vulnerable to fitter male challengers, and to predators. Individual males who are unable to carve out a piece of land for themselves are consigned to bachelor herds – which doesn't mean that they cannot or do not breed, though they do so far less frequently. In the springbok, for instance, territorial behaviour creates a supercharged psychological state that is reflected in enhanced reproductive capacity – an impetus denied the bachelors.

Wildebeest tend to give birth in the hot-wet period – December and January – when the mothers graze on the fresh green grass to produce their nurturing milk. Sometimes though the rains don't come in time, or at all, and many of the calves die. Hartebeest drop their young earlier, usually several weeks before the onset of rain – which is a curiously inappropriate time, for the grazing is at its poorest after the long winter drought. Gemsbok, by contrast, are less predictable in their breeding habits, producing offspring throughout the year though most often during the winter months – and those males without territories do not gather in bachelor groups but, instead, mingle with the females in the breeding herds. The newborn calves, because they appear at different times of the year and, unlike the springbok, cannot rely on numbers for safety, are especially vulnerable to predators. On the other hand, the smallish gemsbok herds are usually scattered over a wider area, and this makes it difficult for the larger carnivores – notably lions and spotted hyaenas – to locate them.

Similarly, eland produce their young over the seasons, peaking between September and December, and, unlike the hartebeest and wildebeest, are not territorial animals: they range too widely to allow the bulls to parcel up the areas. For the first fortnight of their lives – their most vulnerable period – eland calves are hidden away from predators before being grouped together in nursery herds.

Especially intriguing are the reproductive patterns of the Kalahari's springbok, an animal that breeds prolifically – and seems to be able to time its reproductive output to take advantage of favourable conditions (though the precise cue is

THE COURTSHIP OF THE KORHAANS

Among the more spectacular sights in the southern Kalahari is the display flight – a prelude to breeding – of the redcrested korhaan, a medium-sized bird that spends much of its time on the ground, concealed among the low scrubland vegetation. To impress a potential bride it clacks its bill loudly, utters a rising, whistle-like call and runs a short distance before taking off vertically, flying straight up for anything between 10 and 30 metres (11 and 33 yards). It then plunges down, tumbling over and over, its plumage fluffed out, and opens its wings at the last moment to glide elegantly to a resting spot.

*More conspicuous at ground level is its cousin the whitequilled korhaan (**above**), the male of which has an orange bill, yellow legs and white face-patches. The bird can often be seen standing atop a termite mound or other vantage point, and it too has a display flight, a rather less dramatic sequence in which it descends slowly, rather like a particularly noisy little helicopter, squawking loudly, wings flapping rapidly and legs dangling.*

The korhaans are related to the kori bustard, the world's largest flying species, whose great booming call can be heard just before the desert dawn. In display this bird strides about importantly with neck puffed, tail fanned and wings planed and pointed down.

uncertain). This capability accounts for the sudden population explosions of the past and the great springbok treks recorded in the 19th and early 20th centuries.

Each springbok female will give birth to one and, when times are good, two lambs during a 13-month period. Moreover, the lambs within a herd will be born at more or less the same time, a synchronization – a 'flooding of the market', as it were – that cushions the new generation from the predations of spotted hyaenas and other carnivores. The newborn offspring are highly

vulnerable and thus, for the first 20 or so days of their lives, stay hidden away, lying still with head flat to the ground, while the mothers feed some distance away. After three to four weeks, when they are able to run with the adults, they join together in nursery herds tended by mature females.

PREDATOR PARENTS

Some striking examples of distinctive parenting behaviour can also be found among the desert's larger carnivores. Kalahari sci-

entist Gus Mills recalls watching a brown hyaena lift almost half a springbok carcass (a load weighing some 15 kilograms or 33 pounds) and carry it to the cubs in its den a full 10 kilometres (6 miles away). This one happened to be a female, but the males of the species also help nurture the young in this way, even though the cubs that benefit may not be their own. Moreover, the females of the clan will suckle each other's offspring.

Brown hyaenas, though they forage on their own, usually live in loose clans

Above *A bat-eared fox and her pups.*
Following page, left *A spotted hyaena and her offspring.*
Following page, right *The brown hyaena.*

(*see page 105*), but some individual adult males follow a nomadic lifestyle, belonging to no particular association. Curiously, though, these nomads are well received when they wander into a group's territory, so much so that it is they rather than the resident males who will mate with the

females. The intrusion is perfectly acceptable to the males, some of whom will remain celibate for several seasons, seemingly content to contribute to the welfare of the clan (to all of whose members they are related) by helping feed the young.

In a wild dog pack, on the other hand, only the alpha pair – the dominant female and male – are usually permitted to breed and, again, the other members of the extended family renounce their marital rights and serve as helpers, feeding the pups with regurgitated meat brought back from kill or carcass and taking turns to guard the den while the pack hunts. But this arrangement is by no means inflexible: depending on food supplies and the alpha female's tolerance level, a subordinate female is sometimes allowed to mate. Her offsprings' future, though, is hostage to chance: the alpha animal may choose to kill them, or take them over as her own, or simply leave them alone to be reared by their natural mother. Moreover, recent research indicates that, occasionally, a subordinate male also breeds. A wild dog clan's females and males are not related to each other, but there are close same-sex

blood ties – a phenomenon whose origins go back to the formation of the pack, when a single-sex group of dogs left their previous association to seek out a similarly independent group of the opposite sex.

By contrast the mother leopard is a solitary animal, and her cubs – she produces between one and three offspring at any time of the year – are extremely vulnerable to lions and to packs of spotted hyaenas. So she does her best to hide them, in an abandoned antbear hole or in the densest vegetation she can find, and there they remain, silent and immobile, while she is on her hunting forays. Then, every few days, she will move them to a new lair, partly it is thought because the longer they stay in one place the stronger the smell becomes and the more chances there are of detection by a passing predator. After about two months the young are ready to be taken to the kills, and begin hunting for themselves at the age of about eight months, initially taking such small prey as scrub hares and springbok lambs. Leopards, which are fairly common (though elusive) in the Kalahari, are exceptionally resilient animals, largely because of their varied diet.

LIONS AND THEIR YOUNG

Lions, like every other large carnivore, have a tough time of it in the Kalahari. The intense heat forces these big cats to conserve moisture and energy, but at the same time they often have to range far and wide in search of prey. Indeed the desert population tends to live at the outer limit of group viability, in that precarious zone

Above *Cheetah cubs; the number of the park's cheetahs seems to vary in inverse proportion to that of the lions, their main competitors.*
Left *A lioness leads her offspring across the bare veld; cub mortality is high.*
Opposite *A juvenile lion, abandoned by its mother and unlikely to survive.*

where they are only just able to survive. Scarcity of food and the need to move over long distances pose a perennial threat to the very fabric that keeps them together.

Mortality among the young is high – the highest, in fact, in Africa. Cubs have to follow their mothers for huge distances on her wanderings across the sandveld (one monitoring team recorded an eight-week old youngster covering nearly 70 kilometres or 43 miles in just nine days). Exhaustion, starvation and parasitical disease are the biggest killers. Especially starvation: a juvenile lion will remain dependent on its mother for up to 18 months, and if she should fall sick or die during that time its chances of survival are virtually nil.

Other causes of juvenile death include the aggression (sometimes cannibalistic in intent) of the pride's adult male; the predations of spotted hyaenas; the venomous bites of snakes and scorpions and bone disorders related to calcium deficiency. Indeed, females with same-age cubs often get together in prides, or stable maternity groups, partly and perhaps principally in order to lessen the chances of infanticide.

Below *The imperious male lion.*
Right *Lions will copulate with remarkable frequency at mating time, typically at 20-minute intervals over a period of 24 hours or more.*

STRATEGIES FOR DEFENCE

CAMOUFLAGE, MIMICRY, CHEMICAL WARFARE, HORNS AND

THORNS, SECRETIVENESS, FLIGHT, FREEZE, FIGHT, COOPERATION,

THE SAFETY OF NUMBERS — THE MEANS OF SELF-PRESERVATION ARE MANY

AND VARIED; EACH LIFE FORM HAS EVOLVED ITS OWN WAY OF PROTECTING

ITSELF IN ITS DRIVE FOR SPECIES IMMORTALITY.

The carnivorous *oogpister* beetle *Anthia* species, whose name politely translates as the eye-squirter beetle, uses a highly effective weapon when threatened or harassed: it ejects a hot, pungent spray of organic acid that can blind a bird or small mammal. The insect has a black body girdled by a pronounced white stripe that serves as a warning signal to would-be attackers.

There is nothing particularly unusual about the *oogpister's* defence strategy. Many other species – plants, insects and some vertebrates – employ chemicals to protect themselves, though admittedly the *oogpister's* technique is more dramatic than most. All the tenebrionid beetles, for instance, secrete unpleasant and sometimes poisonous fluids over themselves. When attacked by ants or an aardwolf, the snouted harvester termite squirts an irritant substance through a pore at the tip of its snout. But what *is* extraordinary about the *oogpister's* mechanism is the evolutionary

Top *Meerkat constructing bolt-holes.*
Left *The highly toxic African monarch (left) and the monarch mimic (right).*
Right *The pangolin depends on its for-midable armour for self-preservation.*

response it has triggered in an entirely different kind of animal. The young Kalahari sand lizard *Eremias lugubris* is also black with a white stripe, and its stiff-legged, arched-back walking behaviour has more than a passing resemblance to the beetle's gait. The similarity is effective enough to confuse a predator for a second or two – long enough for the lizard to make good its escape. As it grows it develops other means of defence, taking on a duller coloration . and moving in more lizard-like fashion.

Chemical warfare, mimicry, camouflage, armoury, flight, fight, cooperation, the safety of numbers – the strategies for self-preservation are legion: every life form has evolved its own way of protecting itself in its drive for species immortality. Which is pretty self-evident, since without these mechanisms, of course, they could not have avoided extinction.

THE CHEMICAL ARMOURY

Evergreen trees use foul-tasting tannins and phenols to discourage the browsing animals, though they have to strike just the right balance: too high a concentration of these chemicals, known as secondary compounds, will make it difficult for the plant to process life-giving sunlight. Other trees and shrubs have developed similar defences (by contrast, grasses have tough, fibrous stems to inhibit the grazers).

These protective substances, which come in a huge variety of forms, are the evolutionary products of countless battles in the aeons-old war between plant and herbivore. Most are toxic, including the alkaloids; others are not directly poisonous but, instead, serve to reduce the animal's ability to digest its food. When a springbok, eland or other antelope browses on the leaves the tree produces higher levels of the chemicals, and if they are ingested in quantity they will bind up the proteins in the host's rumen and gut, and the animal will effectively starve to death on a full stomach. The herbivores, in turn, have evolved their own defences against this threat, spreading their dietary load among as many trees and tree species as they can.

The desert's geophytes – the corms and bulbs – are especially vulnerable to predation, both above and below ground (among their major subterranean enemies is the mole-rat), for they begin sprouting when the sandveld is at its most barren and their young green shoots are a magnet for the hungry animals. Moreover, unlike shrubs and trees, which are well enough endowed to withstand sustained assault, these plants bear just one stem and very few leaves, so they risk terminal damage from just a single herbivore 'attack'. Thus many geophytes are directly toxic, some armed with especially powerful poisons. In turn, plant-eating mammals and insects have evolved a variety of counter-acting mechanisms, most notably through the operation of what are known as 'mixed-function oxidase' enzymes or MFOs, which provide at least partial and in some cases total immunity. The mole-rat, which

Below *The acid-squirting* oogpister *beetle, with its tell-tale white stripe.*
Opposite, above *The toxic 'poison bulb', one of many Kalahari plant species that have evolved chemical defences.*
Opposite, below *A fake entrance to the Cape penduline tit's nest deceives predators such as snakes.*

The easiest way to escape predation in the wild, of course, is to remain undetected, and a high percentage of animals and not a few plants depend for their survival on avoidance strategies of one sort or another. Most of the small desert vertebrates simply hide away in holes and burrows, and when they do emerge, as they have to in order to feed, they make maximum use of what cover is available. Many others rely to a greater or lesser degree on camouflage, among them some of the 18 recorded species of lizard and gecko, whose coloration renders them barely discernible in their sandy environment. As effective are the colours of such terrestrial birds as the sandgrouse *(see page 54)*, and those of the tiny nocturnal scops owl, which roosts on the stem of a shade tree during the day and whose feathers blend quite beautifully with the bark. To reinforce the deception, the owl changes its distinctive outline by elongating both its body and ear tufts – and hides its large and very recognizable eyes by reducing them to mere slits.

These two types of bird, and indeed nearly every other cryptic desert life form, also employ freeze behaviour because, however ingenious the camouflage, movement will always betray an animal's presence. When approached, the sandgrouse will reveal itself only at the very last moment, flapping away just before it is

cannot afford to be too choosy during its underground foraging forays, is blessed with exceptionally effective MFOs.

Indeed, some wildlife species, especially among the insects, actually feed exclusively on poisonous plants. A few of them, including the African monarch butterfly *Danaus chrysippus*, even extract the toxins from their food and use them to build up their own chemical arsenal.

This on-going arms race between plants and their predators must eventually, one would assume, reach a conclusion: victory for one, defeat for the other. But in fact the war produces neither winners nor losers. Instead a balance is struck. Toxins are costly to produce and store, using up resources that the plant needs to grow and bear seeds, resources which it can ill afford in the unforgiving desert, so it manufactures only what is necessary to achieve browsing

moderation – as opposed to outright prohibition, which would require too heavy an investment in energy and storage capacity.

Based on roughly the same principle but far less complicated are the chemical defences of some vertebrates. The honey badger, for instance, is equipped with anal glands that produce smells offensive enough to intimidate the largest of predators. Kalahari scientist Gus Mills recalls watching four hyaenas chase a badger up a tree. The badger lost its footing and fell down into the pack, and instantly the air was assaulted by a stink as, with teeth bared and rattling, it faced the hyaenas, which jumped away and allowed the badger to disappear into the night. The tiny striped polecat (the males weigh 900 grams or 32 ounces) is similarly armed, the distinctive black and white pattern of its coat warning potential molesters of its noxious weaponry.

trodden on – a behaviour pattern shared by toad grasshoppers. The latter, members of the family Pamphagidae, are masters of disguise, taking on the various shapes and colours of the twigs, stones, leaves and whatever else they rest on. Their common name derives from their short, squat, toad-like bodies. Many animals 'freeze' in order to remain unnoticed. This behaviour brings extra benefits, especially valuable ones in the desert environment: immobility mini-mizes the amount of energy needed for successful escape and, perhaps more importantly, reduces respiratory water loss.

The cryptic approach, though, isn't always designed for defensive purposes. Among other things it plays a prominent part in the hunting strategies of carnivores, enhancing their chances of remaining undetected as they follow or lie in wait for their prey. The buff and black mane of the Kalahari lion blends marvellously into the *driedoring* shrubs and yellow grasses of the Nossob river-bed, and when in stalking mode, with head and body kept close to the ground, the big cat will go unnoticed by even the most cautious of gemsbok.

Opposite, above *The nocturnal and well-camouflaged Bibron's gecko.*
Opposite, below *The leopard's spots merge with the foliage of a tree.*
Above *The Kalahari lion, resplendent with its distinctive black mane.*

The leopard's spots not only merge with the foliage of the tree in which it is resting but provide a degree of camouflage on the more exposed shrublands. Just how important coloration and pattern are to the species is evident from its wide distribution in Africa and southern Asia: hues, appropriate to each different habitat, range from near-white through yellow and brown to almost pure black.

Then there's straightforward mimicry. Spiders are famously deceitful creatures, many adopting the colour and shape of the dry desert grasses in which they live. A select few go a step further and impersonate ants in both appearance – they have the same shape and colour – and, remarkably, in their movements, walking jerkily or raising their front legs to imitate antennae. Just why this should be so has not been established, but it seems to be a device intended to fool the enemy: ants are full of highly unpalatable formic acid, and there is a good chance that look-alikes will be left in peace by spider-eating predators.

The same dynamic drives the non-toxic butterfly *Hypolimnas misippus*, the females of which replicate almost precisely the black, white and orange pattern – the 'aposematic coloration' of many foul-tasting and poisonous insects – of the

feraciously toxic African monarch butter-fly. Even more intriguing, perhaps, is a butterfly known as Bowker's tailed blue, which has evolved a false 'head' complete with 'eyes' and 'antennae', plus a pair of 'forelegs', at the ends of its wings (the 'head' comes together at the rear, when the insect is at rest with its wings folded). The adaptation is, of course, meant to divert the predator's attention away from its real, and vulnerable, front parts.

There are numerous variations on this theme, even among the larger desert life forms. Here the owl again features: the feathers at the back of the pearlspotted owl's head are patterned in the form of a 'face' so that it looks as though the bird is ever-watchful and always fully aware of potential attackers (some butterflies also display bogus eyes, huge ones that stare angrily from the surface of their wings). The whitefaced owl, like the scops, also stretches its body and closes its eyes to alter its all-too-familiar physical character, but uses another piece of deceit when actually threatened: it fluffs its feathers

out, with wings extended and eyes wide open, to appear a lot bigger and fiercer than it really is.

First prize in the false-size stakes, though, must surely go to the innocuous termite-eating aardwolf. This little animal, just 8 kilograms (18 pounds) in weight and equipped with little more than rudi-mentary teeth, erects the long hairs of its mane to increase its bulk, indeed to resemble the fearsome, 60-kilogram (132-pound) spotted hyaena, whose facial fea-tures it shares. It also emits a low-pitched, menacing growl. Similarly, it has been sug-gested that cheetah cubs resemble the honey badger, and thus ride on the latter's well-known and widely respected repu-tation for ferocity.

SHARP ANSWERS

By and large the bigger desert life forms do not depend on deception for security: their visibility, their sheer bulk, precludes camouflage and bluff. Instead they have evolved a variety of sharp protective

projections – thorns in the case of plants (these are known as spinescent species) and horns in ungulates.

Research has shown that the ratio of spinescent to non-spinescent trees and shrubs is higher in arid environments – where ground cover is sparse and there-fore especially vulnerable to herbivores – than in better watered areas. Almost one third of the Kalahari's total plant popula-tion, for instance, bears thorns, which is more than twice the proportion of that of the fynbos vegetation to the south and southwest of the Great Karoo. Every one of the region's acacia species is well endowed with needle-sharp weaponry. Not that this deters the herbivores. It sim-ply slows them down, forces them to be selective, and to work hard for their food. The browser has to manoeuvre its face, lips and tongue to penetrate the spiky mazes; the leaves of many desert species are very small, yielding modest returns for the effort expended; some of the thorns are hooked, which makes it even more dif-ficult for antelope to extricate themselves.

Spines of one sort or another also provide a number of animals with a modicum of protection, though they are often supplementary rather than primary security features. Among those so equipped are the armoured cricket, the girdled lizards (most notably the armadillo variety), and of course the porcupine. The latter seem to be especially favoured by the larger carnivores, no doubt because the fat content of their flesh is high, and their quills are

Right *A thorny acacia branch provides a perch for this purple roller.*
Below *Strength and ferocity are all the defences a lioness usually needs, but these big cats are surprisingly vulnerable to the humble porcupine (**opposite**), whose sharp quills can pierce the flesh and sometimes set up a fatal infection.*

THE ARMOUR-PLATED PANGOLIN

Among the odder looking of the southern Kalahari's residents is the Cape pangolin *Manis temminckii* (**below**), the only living member of the order Pholidota in southern Africa. Ancient in origin, it is unique among the region's mammals in that it is covered, not by hair but by serried ranks of tough, sharp-edged, plate-like scales (**left**).

This formidable coat of armour has helped protect the species from predators for the past 40 million years. It is not, though, the animal's only means of defence. At the merest hint of a threat the pangolin freezes, and in stonier places than the Kalahari is easily overlooked or mistaken for a rock. If detected, it will roll itself up into a tight little ball (**above, right**), covering its face and soft, vulnerable belly. Any attempt to unroll it provokes a vicious scything motion of the tail, whose scales can inflict severe damage to its persecutor's snout and paws. And, if eaten, to its stomach: there is more than a suspicion that at least one Kalahari lion has died, from lacerated guts, after swallowing a pangolin.

The pangolin is a solitary creature, mainly though not entirely nocturnal – it sometimes ventures out on a late winter's afternoon. It spends its active hours foraging for the termites and other insects that make up its diet, locating them by smell and digging them out from beneath the surface of the sandy soil.

frequently put to the test. The porcupine responds to a threat by presenting its bristling back or side to, and thrusting itself at, the attacker.

And, of course, there are the horns of the various antelopes, modestly effective in some, lethal in the case of the gemsbok. The latter confronts its principal desert enemy, the spotted hyaena, by facing head-on to the pack (often with its back against a tree or shrub) and lowering its head so that the long, dagger-sharp horns are level with the ground and chest-high to the predators. It then swings its head from side to side in a dangerous scything motion, and will sometimes launch itself forward in a brief charge. The technique works surprisingly well: in the southern Kalahari, not many more than one in ten hyaena attacks on gemsbok prove successful.

THE HERDING INSTINCT

In general, however, the larger herbivores seek their safety in numbers – in the collective security of herds – rather than in defensive weaponry. Just why gemsbok, eland and wildebeest often gather in big aggregations is the subject of much research and not a little speculation. Defence, it seems, is not the whole answer. But by doing so they certainly enhance their chances of group survival: one calf taken from a herd makes little difference to collective wellbeing. Moreover, herding improves the rate of predator detection, simply because there are more animals to keep watch for potential danger. Here there is an important spin-off benefit: the more eyes there are in a group the more time the herd members can spend feeding. It's interesting to note, in passing, that birds also flock together to visit waterholes – the favoured hunting ground of, among other raptors, the lanner falcons and gabar goshawks – as an anti-predator stratagem. By joining up to drink, otherwise vulnerable laughing doves, for example, spend far less time in being vigilant than they would were they to arrive as individuals.

Right, above The gemsbok's horns are among the deadliest of defensive weapons.
Right Springbok depend on the collective security of the herd, and on fleetness of foot, for survival.

But back to the antelope. Each species reacts to a threat in its own way. Gemsbok, as we have seen, usually face up to the predator with horns at the ready, but will also kick out viciously with their hooves. So too does the eland, largest of the desert herbivores. These animals live in extensive herds which often break up into small groups scattered over a wide area, and defend themselves and their calves by

forming a kind of laager in reverse: they turn inwards, heads together, hindquarters towards the predator – usually a pack of spotted hyaenas – and strike out with their hooves. Among other antelope species, safety is dependent on alertness and, when the danger is perceived, on agility, speed and stamina. In these cases, survival is simply a matter of out-manoeuvring and out-running the opposition.

For a number of reasons the springbok is especially vulnerable to predation, and has developed several protective ploys. Its most distinctive defensive behaviour, though, is its graceful, ballet-like 'pronking', a routine in which the animal literally seems to spring, rather like a pogo-stick, across the veld in a series of 2-metre (7-feet) high leaps – a truly captivating sight. During the sequence the legs remain stiff, the head lowered, the hairs of the white rump fluffed out. Again, the dynamic is not fully understood: pronking carries the animal along at a deceptive pace but not as fast as a gallop, so simple flight cannot be the motivation. Yet the antic must have its uses, and several ideas have been advanced. First, the leaps could confuse a predator who is used to taking its prey on the ground. Then, too, a group of springbok all pronking together might make it difficult for a lion, leopard or hyaena to select a particular individual. The bobbing white rump, moreover, almost certainly acts as an alarm signal, alerting other springbok in the area, and sends a message to the carnivore, saying 'I've seen you'. Finally, pronking enhances vigilance, giving each member of a herd a clear view of the surrounding countryside and its lurking dangers.

The cooperative approach

Some animals – most notably the suricate, or meerkat *(see page 91)* – depend heavily for self-preservation on cooperative effort within the group.

Meerkats are in the ambivalent position of being both predator and prey. They spend the days digging furiously with their front claws for the insects, grubs, geckos, scorpions and the huge and seemingly unappetizing Kalahari millipedes that, together, make up their diet – which means that, for much of the time, their heads are buried in the sand, making them highly vulnerable to both the hovering raptor and the ground-living hunter. So the species has evolved an elaborate and remarkably sophisticated early-warning system. Or rather, two systems, both based on close cooperation.

First, some of the meerkats – often the subadults of and immigrants to the group – stop foraging every few seconds to sit bolt upright on their hind legs to peer up at the sky and survey the surroundings for signs of danger, and sound the alarm when they see or suspect a threat. Interestingly, the interval between work-breaks varies with the size of the group: again, the larger the number of members, and therefore the greater the number of eyes and ears, the longer the time each individual can spend foraging without interruption.

The meerkats will, however, give their undivided attention to the search for food when the second system gears in. This involves the posting of a full-time sentinel, an individual who stops work completely to sit, with head erect and front paws held out, on a tree-stump, termite mound or some other convenient vantage point to keep a careful eye on the area. Throughout its tour of duty the sentry makes a soft, regular, chirping sound which signals that all is well. If the noise ceases, the rest will know something is wrong. On the other hand if it spots a predator in time, it will give either a short bark, which denotes a bird of prey (the tawny and martial eagles are the most feared of their enemies), or a hoot, which identifies a terrestrial threat, whereupon the whole group flees to the nearest shelter.

These defensive systems occasionally break down, notably in times of drought or when the group size drops below a critical point and the need for food outweighs the

Left *The springbok's high leaps, and its 'pronking', signal agility and elusiveness to would-be predators.*
Above *Speed and cryptic coloration provide the cheetah's defences.*

need for vigilance. Moreover, predators do manage to get close, even with a sentry posted, and sometimes there's no cover nearby. A jackal, perhaps, will venture onto the scene, and on these occasions the meerkats will crowd together, rock backwards and forwards with their fur raised and their mouths agape, and then launch themselves, in one sinuous, writhing mass, at the intruder. The latter is very often intimidated and backs off. Although meerkats are marvellously cooperative within their own groups, they treat neighbouring ones with outright and unreserved hostility. They are highly territorial animals, scent-marking their patches frequently, defecating collectively near the territory's boundary, and when another band of

Above *Safety in numbers.*
Left *Stealth and strength epitomized.*
Right *Meerkats have remarkably sharp eyes: they can differentiate between a dangerous martial eagle and a less threatening snake eagle at a distance of 2 kilometres (1.2 miles).*

meerkats approaches they again bunch up to leap about in a kind of war dance, posturing and kicking up the dust in a display of strength. They then mount a frontal assault. The larger group invariably wins the battle, celebrates with a great deal of congratulary behaviour and, in all too human fashion, often attracts deserters from the routed enemy.

CHALLENGES FOR THE FUTURE

ALL OVER AFRICA THE SPACES STILL AVAILABLE TO THE

WILDLIFE ARE SHRINKING, AND THE CONTINENT'S PARKS HAVE

BECOME ISLANDS IN AN OCEAN OF HUMAN ENCROACHMENT.

THE KALAHARI'S SCIENTISTS ARE IN THE VANGUARD

OF THE CONSERVATION CAMPAIGN.

The countryside extending away to the south of the Kalahari Gemsbok National Park is for the most part featureless, monochromatic, desolate in its huge emptiness. Its great semi-desert spaces are sparsely populated; signs of life, any kind of life, are few and far between. But here and there is the occasional, isolated farmhouse; one or two tarred highways run straight as arrows to distant horizons; lesser, gravel-surfaced routes crisscross the sandveld to connect tiny, infinitely remote hamlets.

Yet there is an odd sense of confinement as you drive through the region, a feeling created by the power lines, the water pipes and, above all, by the myriad fences that line the roads and the borders of the spacious properties. The fences represent the single most important tool in livestock management – and the one element most responsible for the destruction of the region's wildlife. To the north of the park, on the Botswana side of the southern Kalahari, there are fewer fences. But the mere presence of people, together with all the things they do to ensure

---

Top *Ground squirrels befriend a visitor at Mata Mata.*
Above *The Cape turtle dove, a familiar presence at camps and waterholes.*
Right *A dead camelthorn, victim of a lightning strike, stands stark in the Nossob valley.*

their survival and enhance their economic wellbeing, acts as another kind of barrier.

In short, the open plains of the southern Kalahari, once home to vast herds of migrating herbivores and their trailing predators, have undergone radical change: only in the national parks has something like their original character been preserved, so these conservancies are akin to pristine islands in an ocean of spoliation. Moreover, even though the parks successfully sustain much of the region's precious fauna and flora – with some notable exceptions, such as the wild dog – they do so on

a limited scale and thus, with the reduction in the size of the wildlife populations, there is a progressive decline in genetic interchange and genetic diversity (a case in point is the status of the Kalahari's lions: a recent, though preliminary, survey shows

Left *A red hartebeest; in seasons of good rains 1 000 and more of these large antelope will gather in the Nossob valley.* Below *The hot, dry, dust-laden winds that sweep over the desert often provoke snake and scorpion activity.*

the population to be genetically deficient, which may well be a consequence of isolation and inbreeding). This, for the biologist and the environmental manager, represents perhaps the most testing challenge.

The contraction of the wilderness poses another threat, a more insidious, arguably even more dangerous one, for by their very existence, their special status, the conservation areas have been alienated from the rural communities and the role of the two southern Kalahari parks in human society, like that of other parks throughout Africa, is being questioned. Could not these

conservancies, people ask, be more profitably used if given over to cattle and sheep? Why do they have to be so large; could they not provide the same wilderness experience if they were half their size? Why can't the game be commercially exploited through hunting and cropping? Why does southern Africa have so many parks and reserves; aren't the Kruger, the Chobe and the Etosha big enough to meet the demands of conservation? And, the most crucial question of all: are we not more concerned with protecting animals than with helping human beings?

THE PRICELESS LEGACY

Most of Africa's more extensive conservation areas were originally set aside to protect the bigger, more charismatic animals – elephants, rhino, the antelope herds and the larger carnivores. In the event this proved a blessing, for by their very nature and size these species demand a lot of living room, and the resultant spaciousness has enabled much else – other forms of life that, in earlier days, either went unnoticed or were discounted as insignificant – to survive. Only fairly recently has the importance of biodiversity, the need to conserve *all* organisms, been fully appreciated by scientists and, increasingly, by the decision makers and general public. It is now accepted that human society is still surprisingly dependent on the natural order and will remain so far into the future for, among other things, its food and medicines. In fact we need even greater biodiversity to ensure our long-term welfare – to enable us, for instance, to fight crop diseases and agricultural pests, to develop new types of standard crops through interbreeding with wild strains.

Nevertheless, the biodiversity argument remains meaningless to the people on the ground. To them, conservation efforts are irrelevant unless they yield direct recreational, educational and, above all,

Left *Once or twice a year spider webs, carried by strong winds, adorn plant and animal alike.*
Above *A rare sight in the Kalahari – this warthog was seen near Twee Rivieren.*
Below *Jackal at sunrise.*

financial rewards. So the challenge is to build in these incentives, and in this context a significant trend has emerged over recent years. There is, today, a general realization that the wellbeing of wildlife and the interests of tourism need not be in conflict with the needs of the rural

Above *Scientists radio-tracking the progress of a honey badger. The other desert animals are similarly monitored. Seasonal aerial surveys keep count of large-mammal populations.*
Left *The hide at Nossob camp.*

communities, and a new kind of park has made its appearance, an integrated area in which the people of the countryside, instead of being excluded or relocated, stay where they are, identify with and help protect the environment, share in its resources – and, at the same time, benefit from tourism development.

This last element is becoming increasingly important as government budget allocations decline (a worldwide phenomenon). Parks and reserves throughout the subcontinent are under mounting pressure to pay their own way ('if it pays, it stays' is the increasingly quoted maxim, and a potentially destructive one it is, too);

THE CUTTING EDGE

There is some evidence – circumstantial but fairly strong – that the red dune country of the southern Kalahari once sustained healthy numbers of giraffe. Be that as it may, they are certainly there now, introduced as part of a research programme. In 1990 eight of these elegant, super-tall creatures (**right and below**) were translocated from Namibia's Etosha park and accommodated in a 14,8 square-kilometre (5.7-mile²), fenced and predator-free area near Mata Mata. Their number has since increased to 14, and in due course they will be released to fend for themselves in the dunelands, where there is suitable browse. If they do well, more will probably be brought in.

The harsh, waterless desert environment offers exciting opportunities for research, especially into animal survival strategies, and the giraffe programme is just one of about 70 projects scientists are conducting within the Kalahari Gemsbok National Park. They are all different, but together they will help fulfil two broad and related aims: the preservation of the region's biodiversity, and the maintenance of its fragile ecosystem. The latter involves, among other things, intense study of the dramatic changes that take place in the dune vegetation, and their effect on animal movement patterns and population cycles. Among the more prominent of the projects is the long-term monitoring of numbers and movement through regular aerial counts - surveys that quantify the park's migrant as well as its permanent herds (maximum migrant numbers total 170 000 wildebeest, 18 000 red hartebeest and 13 000 eland). Other studies focus on the key role of the camelthorn tree within the ecosystem, the dynamics of the Kalahari's lion community, and the mating strategies of tenebrionid beetles. The most closely studied of the Kalahari's animals is the meerkat, or suricate.

conservation authorities become more and more preoccupied with promoting eco-tourism, with raising funds through the award of hunting and safari concessions and with other endeavours that can, if not properly planned and controlled, have a detrimental, even devastating impact on the environment. This, in turn, would damage tourism potential. As a consequence, emphasis is now being placed on subdividing the parks, creating separate mass-tourism, minimum-use and no-go (specially protected) zones in an effort to strike a balance – between, on the one hand, the commercial imperatives and, on the other, the need to preserve the wildlife, the peace and the beauty of the land.

Much of this thinking is reflected in the administration, by the joint transfrontier committee (see page 31), of the two south-ern Kalahari parks. Saloon cars, for exam-ple, are allowed only along the Nossob and Auob river-beds and the two roads linking them; the dune areas are accessible only via low-impact four-wheel-drive trails; much of the remainder of the region is maintained as strictly protected wilder-ness; hunting is forbidden, activity limited to what officialdom calls 'non-consumptive utilization' (camera safaris).

If this were all, the parks would still be vulnerable, the object of scepticism among the poor people of the surrounding

Botswana park have been classed (though, at the time of writing, the communities were still to give their formal approval) as wildlife management areas in which both the local folk and high-paying visitors are allowed to hunt the 'overflow' of animals. Much the same arrangement could be introduced on the South African side by incorporating the present hunting camps (in the adjacent Mier community area) into the parks system, a move that would allow access to a greater number and variety of species. In short, as an alternative to the pernicious game fences, the development of the parks should and hopefully will be geared in with that of the neighbouring countryside to produce a smooth gradation from wildlife to livestock. Among further options is the future of the remnant =Khomani Bushmen within the South African park. Such a translocation would benefit both the community and the conservation effort (a section of the Bushmen community has long and skilfully served as rangers and research assistants). It is doubtful, though, whether the move would also preserve Bushman identity. Closer contact with outsiders and an enhanced earning capacity are more likely to accelerate the erosion of traditional culture.

Above *Gemsbok spoor on the dunes.*
Right, above *Visitors trail a lioness.*
Right *Two male siblings are joyfully reunited near Nossob camp after being apart for a few days.*

countryside. The task therefore is to integrate the two sectors of interest.

A start has already been made: large tracts of sandveld just outside the

VISITORS' ADVISORY

The Kalahari Gemsbok National Park has three rest-camps, largest of which is Twee Rivieren, located at the junction of the Nossob and Auob rivers in the south. Facilities here comprise 31 airconditioned, modern, self-catering, fully equipped chalets, 30 camp sites, a pleasant restaurant, a swimming pool and an information centre. The older established Nossob camp, 160 kilometres (99 miles) upriver from Twee Rivieren, offers ten fully equipped (6- and 3-bed) self-catering huts and a floodlit game hide. Mata Mata, the smallest venue (five units and 20 camp sites) is set on the bank of the invariably dry Auob River on the Namibian border to the west. Information centres are planned for both Nossob and Mata Mata.

Each camp has a grocery shop, though only Twee Rivieren's stocks fresh goods (meat, bread, margarine, eggs). Alcoholic beverages, barbecue firewood and petrol are also on sale. A new, privately managed tented camp, sited in the lower Auob river-bed, was scheduled for completion in 1997.

Getting there: By road from South Africa: via Upington, 286 kilometres (178 miles) to the south. Some 170 kilometres (106 miles) of the route is tarred. By road from Namibia: via Keetmanshoop, Aroab and Rietfontein to Andriesville. Petrol is available at the camps. By air: Twee Rivieren has a registered landing strip, and an Avis car hire service.

Getting around: The game-viewing roads follow the courses of the Auob and Nossob rivers; two dune tracks link the Auob and Nossob river-beds. There are five picnic spots within the game territory. None is fenced; motorists alight from their vehicles at their own risk. Some stretches of road may be difficult to negotiate during the rainy season.

Visitors should not stray from the established routes (vehicles can easily come to grief in the soft sands) and are asked to inform the camp office of their itinerary before setting out.

Lists of mammals, birds, reptiles, amphibians and flora are available at the camps.

The Gemsbok National Park, on the Botswana side, is not well developed for tourism. Visitor amenities amount to just two camp sites (no facilities provided; bring your own food and bedding) at Rooiputs and Grootbrak along the Nossob River and Polenswa tributaries respectively. Access from Botswana is from Tsabong or Boksputs. Easier access to the Botswana park is the subject of negotiation within the transfrontier committee.

Reservations: in advance through the central booking office, Tel. (012) 343 1991, fax (012) 343 0905; or through the regional (Cape Town) office, Tel. (021) 22 2810, fax (021) 24 6211.

THE GROWING HUMAN PRESENCE

Tourism to the Kalahari Gemsbok National Park has increased markedly in recent years – from 17 800 to 28 000 visitors during the first half of the 1990s. And, with the completion of the tarred road to the south of Twee Rivieren, the numbers will continue climbing. Moreover, the transfrontier arrangement is likely to lead to the commercial development of the Botswana park. Tourism in the wider area will also be boosted by the new trans-Kalahari highway running from the Botswana capital, Gaborone, westwards into neighbouring Namibia.

Thus the two parks are set fair to contribute a great deal more to the economy of an arid, historically poor region. But somehow, in doing so, they must fulfil their proper function and continue to preserve the sandveld plains, their nomadic herds, and their unique ecosystem.

Above *Leopard at rest.*
Right *Cheetah in lively mood.*

SIGNS IN THE SAND

The Kalahari's terrain, with its soft, sandy surfaces and sparse wildlife, is ideal tracking ground. Spoor are clearly visible, their characteristic shapes retained in recognizable form long after the animal has passed. The illustrations on these two pages represent the footprints that the desert's more prominent species leave behind them. (1 centimetre = 0.3937 inches)

CARNIVORES

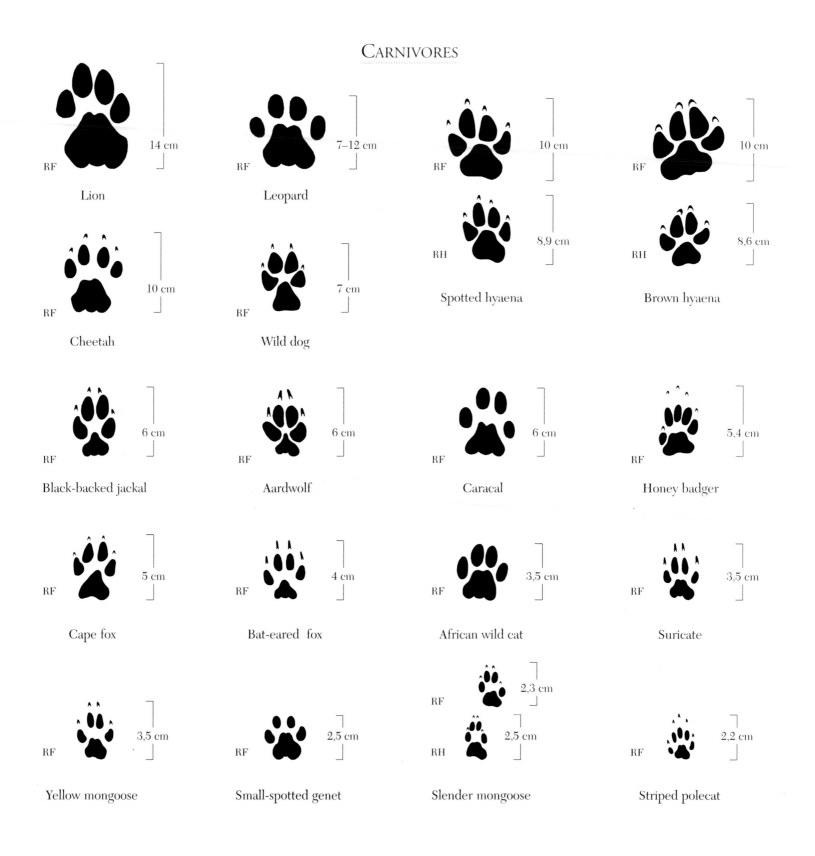

RF — 14 cm — Lion

RF — 7–12 cm — Leopard

RF — 10 cm — Spotted hyaena
RH — 8,9 cm — Spotted hyaena

RF — 10 cm — Brown hyaena
RH — 8,6 cm — Brown hyaena

RF — 10 cm — Cheetah

RF — 7 cm — Wild dog

RF — 6 cm — Black-backed jackal

RF — 6 cm — Aardwolf

RF — 6 cm — Caracal

RF — 5,4 cm — Honey badger

RF — 5 cm — Cape fox

RF — 4 cm — Bat-eared fox

RF — 3,5 cm — African wild cat

RF — 3,5 cm — Suricate

RF — 3,5 cm — Yellow mongoose

RF — 2,5 cm — Small-spotted genet

RF — 2,3 cm — Slender mongoose
RH — 2,5 cm — Slender mongoose

RF — 2,2 cm — Striped polecat

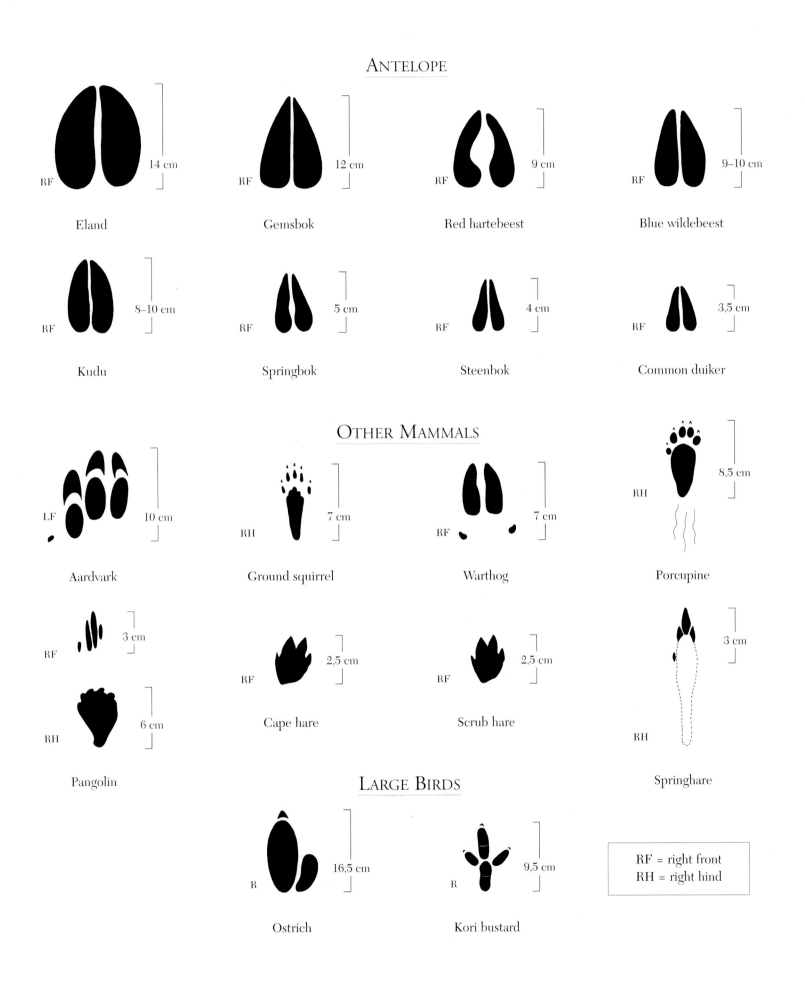

ANTELOPE

Eland — RF — 14 cm

Gemsbok — RF — 12 cm

Red hartebeest — RF — 9 cm

Blue wildebeest — RF — 9–10 cm

Kudu — RF — 8–10 cm

Springbok — RF — 5 cm

Steenbok — RF — 4 cm

Common duiker — RF — 3,5 cm

OTHER MAMMALS

Aardvark — LF — 10 cm

Ground squirrel — RH — 7 cm

Warthog — RF — 7 cm

Porcupine — RH — 8,5 cm

Pangolin — RF — 3 cm, RH — 6 cm

Cape hare — RF — 2,5 cm

Scrub hare — RF — 2,5 cm

Springhare — RH — 3 cm

LARGE BIRDS

Ostrich — R — 16,5 cm

Kori bustard — R — 9,5 cm

RF = right front
RH = right hind

INDEX

CHECKLIST: COMMON WILDLIFE

The following is a select list of the more prominent and visible plants, reptiles, birds and mammals recorded within the Kalahari Gemsbok National Park.

PLANTS

Acacia, candle- *Acacia hebeclada*
Asparagus, wild *Asparagus* spp.
Bloubos (skaapbossie) *Monechma incanum*
Brandy bush *Grewia flava*
Broom bush *Crotalaria spartioides*
Chloris, feather top *Chloris virgata*
Cluster-leaf, silver *Terminalia sericea*
Cucumber, gemsbok *Acanthosicyos naudinianus*
    wild *Cucumis africanus*
Devil's claw *Harpagophytum procumbens*
Driedoring *Rhigozum trichotomum*
Dubbeltjie *Tribulus zeyheri*,
Dubbeltjie *T. terrestris*

Ganna bush *Salsola rabieana*
Grass, bristle-burr *Setaria verticillata*
    buffalo *Panicum coloratum*
    gemsbok *Eragrostis pallens*
    gha *Centropodia glauca*
    Kalahari *Schmidtia kalahariensis*
    love *Eragrostis lehmanniana*
    short bushman *Stipagrostis obtusa*
    speckled vlei *Eragrostis bicolor*
    tall bushman *Stipagrostis ciliata*
Lily, vlei- *Nerine laticoma*
Perdebos *Monechma genistifolium*
Poison bulb *Boophane disticha*
Poppy, Mexican *Argemone subfusiformis*
Reed, dune- *Stipagrostis amabilis*
Sewejaartjie *Helichrysum argyrosphaerum*
Springbokopslag *Indigofera alternans*
Swartstorm *Senna italica*
Taaibos, Kalahari *Rhus tenuinervis*
Thorn, bastard umbrella *Acacia luederitzii*

    black- *A. mellifera*
    camel- *A. erioloba*
    grey camel- *A. haematoxylon*
Tree, Shepherd's *Boscia albitrunca*
    wild green-hair *Parkinsonia africana*
Truffle, Kalahari *Terfezia* spp.
Tsamma melon *Citrullus lanatus*
Volstruisdruiwe *Gisekia africana*
Wattle, eland's *Elephantorrhiza elephantina*

REPTILES

Adder, horned *Bitis caudalis*
Agama, ground *Agama aculeata aculeata*
Boomslang *Dispholidus typus typus*
Cobra, Cape *Naja nivea*
Egg eater, common *Dasypeltis scabra*
Chamaeleon, flap-necked *Chamaeleon Chamaeleo dilepis*
Gecko, Bibron's *Pachydactylus bibronii*
    Cape dwarf *Lygodactylus capensis capensis*

    Cape *Pachydactylus capensis*
    common barking *Ptenopus garrulus garrulus*
    giant ground *Chondrodactylus angulifer angulifer*
    Kalahari ground *Colopus wahlbergii furcifer*
    rough-scaled *Pachydactylus rogusus rogusus*
    speckled *Pachydactylus punctatus*
Lizard, bushveld *Heliobolus lugubris*
    Cape spade-snouted worm *Monopeltis capensis capensis*
    common rough-scaled *Ichnotropis squamulosa*
    Kalahari round-headed worm *Zygaspis quadrifrons*
    Kalahari sand *Eremias lugubris*
    Namaqua sand *Pedioplanis namaquensis*
    slender spade-snouted worm *Monopeltis sphenorhynchus mauricei*
    spotted sand *Pedioplanis lineoocellata lineoocellata*
    striped sandveld *Nucras tessellata tessellata*

Monitor, rock *Varanus exanthematicus albigularis*
Puff adder *Bitis arietans*
Skink, Cape *Mabuya capensis*
  Kalahari tree *Mabuya spilogaster*
  striped *Mabuya striata sparsa*
  variegated *Mabuya variegata variegata*
  Western three-striped *Mabuya occidentalis*
Snake, Karoo sand *Psammophis notostictus*
  fork-marked sand *Psammophis leightoni trinasalis*
  mole *Pseudaspis cana*
Terrapin, marsh *Pelomedusa subrufa*
Tortoise, leopard *Geochelone pardalis*
  serrated/Kalahari tent *Psammobates oculifer*

AMPHIBIA

Caco, common *Cacosternum boettgeri*
Frog, giant bull *Pyxicephalus adspersus*
  bushveld rain- *Breviceps adspersus adspersus*
  Tremolo sand *Tomopterna cryptotis*
Toad, olive *Bufo garmani*

BIRDS

Barbet, pied *Lybius leucomelas*
Bateleur *Terathopius ecaudatus*
Batis, pririt *Batis pririt*
Bee-eater, swallowtailed *Merops hirundineus*
Bokmakierie *Telophorus zeylonus*
Brubru *Nilaus afer*
Bulbul, redeyed *Pycnonotus nigricans*
Bustard, Kori *Ardeotis kori*
  Ludwig's *Neotis ludwigii*
Buzzard, Steppe *Buteo buteo*
Canary, yellow *Serinus flaviventris*
Chat, anteating *Myrmecocichla formicivora*
  familiar *Cercomela familiaris*
  desert *Cisticola aridula*
Courser, doublebanded *Rhinoptilus africanus*
Crow, black *Corvus capensis*
Dikkop, spotted *Burhinus capensis*
Dove, Cape turtle *Streptopelia capicola*
  laughing *Streptopelia senegalensis*
  Namaqua *Oena capensis*

Drongo, forktailed *Dicrurus adsimilis*
Eagle, blackbreasted snake *Circaetus gallicus*
Eagle, booted *Hieraaetus pennatus*
  brown snake *Circaetus cinereus*
  martial *Polemaetus bellicosus*
  Steppe *Aquila nipalensis*
  tawny *Aquila rapax*
  Wahlberg's *Aquila pomarina*
Eremomela, yellowbellied *Eremomela icteropygialis*
Falcon, lanner *Falco biarmicus*
  pygmy *Polihierax semitorquatus*
  rednecked *Falco chicquera*
Finch, scalyfeathered *Sporopipes squamifrons*
Flycatcher, chat *Melaenornis infuscatus*
  Marico *Melaenornis mariquensis*
Goshawk, gabar *Micronisus gabar*
  pale chanting *Melierax canorus*
Hornbill, yellowbilled *Tockus flavirostris*
Kestrel, greater *Falco rupicoloides*
  lesser *Falco naumanni*
  rock *Falco tinnunculus*
Kite, blackshouldered *Elanus caeruleus*
  yellowbilled (black) *Milvus migrans*
Korhaan, redcrested *Eupodotis ruficrista*
  white-quilled (black) *Eupodotis afraoides*
Lark, clapper *Mirafra apiata*
  fawncolored *Mirafra africanoides*
  Sabota *Mirafra sabota*
Martin, rock *Hirundo fuligula*
Ostrich *Struthio camelus*
Owl, African scops *Otus senegalensis*
  barn *Tyto alba*
  giant eagle *Bubo lacteus*
  pearlspotted *Glaucidium perlatum*
  spotted eagle *Bubo africanus*
  whitefaced *Otus leucotis*
Plover, blacksmith *Vanellus armatus*
  crowned *Vanellus coronatus*
Prinia, blackchested *Prinia flavicans*
Robin, Kalahari *Erythropygia paena*
Roller, lilacbreasted *Coracias caudata*
Sandgrouse, Burchell's *Pterocles burchelli*
  Namaqua *Pterocles namaqua*

Scimitarbill, Greater *Phoeniculus rhinopomastus*
Secretary bird *Sagittarius serpentarius*
Shrike, crimsonbreasted *Laniarius atrococcineus*
  fiscal *Lanius collaris*
Sparrow, Cape *Passer melanurus*
  house *Passer domesticus*
Sparrow-weaver, whitebrowed *Plocepasser mahali*
Starling, Burchell's *Lamprotornis australis*
  glossy *Lamprotornis nitens*
Stork, Abdim's *Ciconia abdimii*
  black *Ciconia nigra*
  white *Ciconia ciconia*
Swallow, European *Hirundo rustica*
  South African cliff *Hirundo spilodera*
  whitethroated *Hirundo albigularis*
Tit, Cape penduline *Anthoscopus minutus*
  southern grey *Parus afer*
Titbabbler *Parisoma subcaeruleum*
Vulture, Cape *Gyps coprotheres*
  hooded *Necrosyrtes monachus*
  lappetfaced *Torgos tracheliotus*
  whitebacked *Gyps africanus*
  whiteheaded *Trigonoceps occipitalis*
Weaver, masked *Ploceus velatus*
  redbilled buffalo *Bubalornis niger*
  sociable *Philetairus socius*
Wheatear, capped *Oenanthe pileata*
Whydah, shaft-tailed *Vidua regia*
Woodpecker, cardinal *Dendropicos fuscescens*

MAMMALS

Aardvark/Antbear *Orycteropus afer*
Aardwolf *Proteles cristatus*
Baboon, Chacma *Papio cynocephalus ursinus*
Caracal *Felis caracal*
Cat, African wild *Felis lybica*
Cheetah *Acinoyx jubatus*
Dassie, rock *Procavia capensis*
Duiker, Common *Sylvicapra grimmia*
Eland *Taurotragus oryx*
Elephant-shrew, bushveld *Elephantulus intufi*
  round-eared *Macroscelides proboscideus*
Fox, bat-eared *Otocyon megalotis*

  Cape *Vulpes chama*
Gemsbok *Oryx gazella*
Genet, small-spotted *Genetta genetta*
Gerbil, hairy-footed *Gerbillurus paeba*
  short-tailed *Desmodillus auricularis*
Giraffe *Giraffa camelopardalis*
Hare, Cape *Lepus capensis*
  scrub *Lepus saxatilis*
Hartebeest, red *Alcelaphus buselaphus*
Hedgehog, South African *Atelerix frontalis*
Honey badger *Mellivora capensis*
Hyaena, brown *Hyaena brunnea*
  spotted *Crocuta crocuta*
Impala *Aepyceros melampus*
Jackal, black-backed *Canis mesomelas*
Kudu *Tragelaphus strepsiceros*
Leopard *Panthera pardus*
Lion *Panthera leo*
Meerkat (Suricate) *Suricata suricatta*
Mole, Cape golden *Chrysochloris asiatica*
Molerat, Damara *Cryptomys damarensis*
Mongoose, banded *Mungos mungo*
  slender *Herpestes sanguinea*
  yellow *Cynictis penicillata*
Mouse, grey climbing *Dendromus melanotis*
  large-eared *Malacothrix typica*
  Namaqua rock *Aethomys namaquensis*
  pouched *Saccostomus campestris*
  pygmy *Mus minutoides*
  striped *Rhabdomys pumilio*
Pangolin *Manis temminckii*
Polecat, striped *Ictonyx striatus*
Porcupine *Hystrix africaeaustralis*
Rat, black-tailed tree *Thallomys nigricauda*
  Brants' whistling *Parotomys brantsii*
  Woosnam's desert *Zelotomys woosnami*
Shrew, lesser red musk *Crocidura hirta*
Springbok *Antidorcas marsupialis*
Springhare *Pedetes capensis*
Squirrel, Cape ground *Xerus inauris*
Steenbok *Raphicerus campestris*
Warthog *Phacochoerus aethiopicus*
Wild dog *Lycaon pictus*
Wildebeest, blue *Connochaetes taurinus*

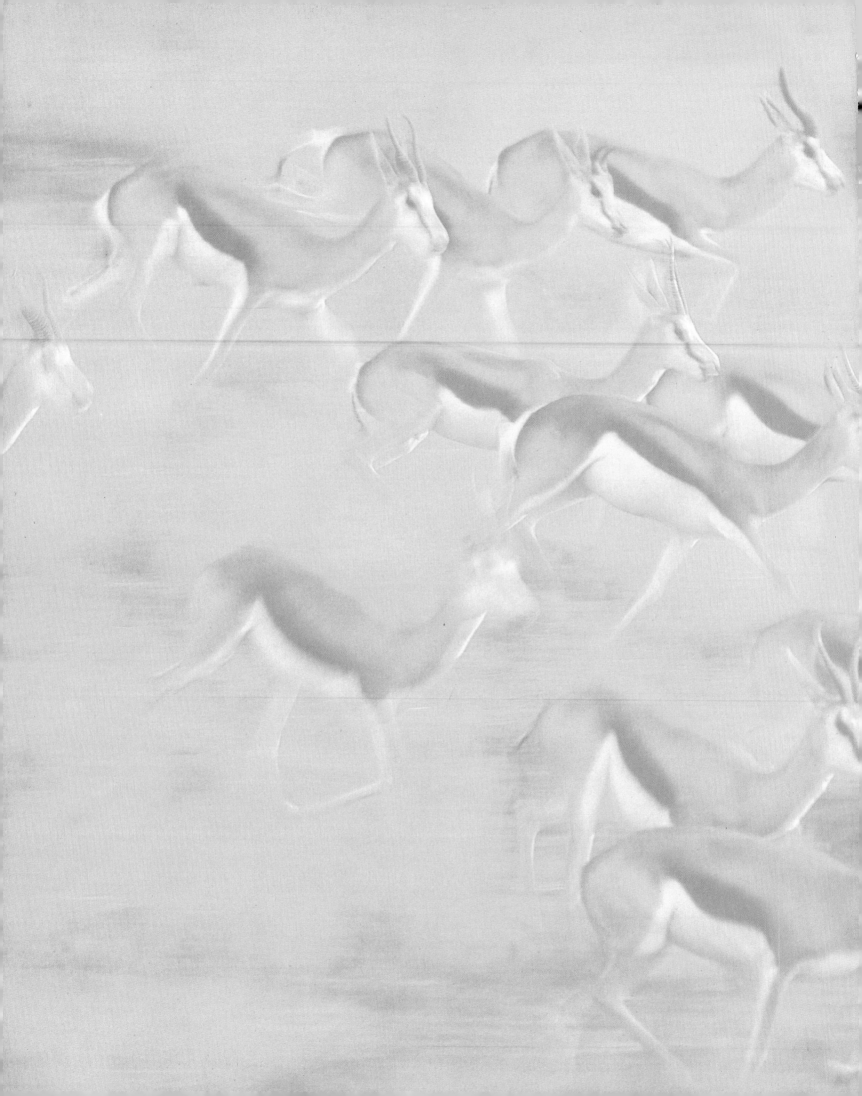